The Seven Habits Of Peaceful Parents

A Facilitator's Manual

Dr. Joseph Cress
Dr. Elizabeth Lonning
Burt Berlowe

Resource Publications, Inc.
San Jose, California

Acknowledgments

This book represents the contributions and experiences of many people. We would like to acknowledge several who have made special contributions. Rebecca Janke, of Growing Communities for Peace, has been a source of inspiration and encouragement from the outset. Julie Walker bore the brunt of manuscript preparation. She cheerfully helped us meet our deadlines. Kenneth Guentert, our editor, was insightful, supportive, and very helpful. The local chapter of the National Committee for the Prevention of Child Abuse was also supportive. Robert Cress critically read the manuscript and provided valuable feedback. Finally, our clients, children, and parents have taught us a great deal about peaceful and compassionate parenting.

Introduction

*P*eaceful parenting evolved as a way to help parents become familiar with basic skills and to use them first and foremost within their own families. A peaceful family is more than one that has no violence or conflict. Peaceful family life is exciting and expansive. It embraces togetherness, a sense of connection, action, accomplishment, and joy. As parents and families explore the meaning of peace, they can create safe and harmonious homes where all members can grow to the fullest and begin to combat the violent tendencies in our larger culture.

Throughout history, little formal training has been available to prepare men and women to be parents. For years, societies have trained and licensed people to practice medicine, dentistry, or law. Even in an era of technological advances, not much has been done to prepare parents for the tough task of rearing children. We teach prospective parents child-birthing techniques, but those classes don't tell them how to deal with the child after he or she is born. Although many communities offer parenting classes, few moms and dads attend them. The result is that even now, as in times gone by, children are still being abused in one form or another.

That's why we developed this training manual to accompany *The Peaceful Parenting Handbook*. It will give parents an opportunity to continue learning beyond an initial reading, workshop, or class and to pass that knowledge on to others who need it.

This training manual, supplemented by *The Peaceful Parenting Handbook*, addresses these issues. Using the information here, parents will be able to expand their discipline options and child development skills, manage anger, enhance their family relationships, and attain the ultimate goal of raising peaceful children.

Our goal with this manual is to train professionals and parents to continue and expand the work that we now do. Perhaps someday soon, you can help us teach parents how to raise their children the peaceful way.

Part One

In the Beginning

Peaceful Parenting

*P*sychologists believe aggressive behavior and violence evolve primarily from home and family life. In general, harsh physical punishment, parental rejection, excessive restriction, and exposure to vivid filmed violence seem to lead to violence and aggression, perpetuating the cycle from one generation to the next. Given this perspective, family educators must develop specific strategies to enhance and promote peaceful parenting and peaceful families.

In fact, this has been happening. In the last half of the twentieth century, educators and psychologists have developed a few formal training programs, each one insisting that this is "the right way" to parent. Progressive educators have promoted child-rearing philosophies that focus on training and guidance, rather than on rigid punishment.

In general, however, little formal training has been available to prepare men and women to be parents. For years, societies have trained and licensed people to practice medicine, dentistry, or law. But even in an era of high technological advances, relatively little has been done to prepare parents for the task of raising children. We teach prospective parents child-birthing techniques but don't tell them how to deal with the child after he or she is born. While many communities offer parenting classes, few moms and dads attend them. The result is that even now, as in bygone times, children are being abused with alarming frequency.

Peaceful parenting has blossomed as an active and creative problem-solving approach to child rearing that focuses on positive, well-established alternatives to violent and aversive parenting approaches. It promotes self-control and self-esteem in the children as well as in the parents. Peaceful parenting relies on active listening and empathic responding. It encompasses a unique set of feelings, values, attitudes, and skills. Ultimately, it's a means of acquainting parents with the insight and skills they need to meet their own goals for their children in a peaceful, effective fashion.

Peaceful parenting also challenges family educators to expand and stretch their ways of teaching current and future parents, so that a peaceful family life can be active, creative, joyous, and enriching. And, as parents and families explore the meaning of peace, they will create safe and harmonious homes where all members can enjoy life and grow to their fullest potential.

In the years since we published our book *Peaceful Parenting in a Violent World*, we have met, talked with, and educated hundreds of parents from all kinds of families, cultures, and income levels. We have also educated day care providers, teachers, social workers, and others in the caregiving field. Our contacts with them have evoked a variety of concerns and questions. But they all shared a yearning for ways to bring up children peacefully in our violent world.

This adventure has given us many rewards: primarily the satisfaction of helping adults work through their child development issues while building a more peaceful world for the next generation. At the same time, there have been frustrations. We have not been able to get peaceful parenting information to those who need it the most, but who do not have the resources necessary to attend a class, buy a book, or join a support group. Although we have connected with many parents in hardship situations, there are so many more we have not reached. Another frustration has been that we have no way of knowing what happens to the families we work with after our job is done. Have they used or benefited from peaceful parenting? In both instances, we fear that many parents have been left to fend for themselves without the training they need to succeed.

These recent experiences have given us cause for both hope and concern. We are encouraged by the efforts of many parents and professionals who are practicing peaceful parenting and spreading the word to others. Despite this good work, however, the incidence of child abuse continues to grow. For one reason or another, adults who have not yet heard or heeded the peaceful parenting message continue to abuse their children—sometimes with sticks or fists, often without lifting a finger.

Why does this happen? There are two primary reasons children are abused. The first reason is lack of parenting knowledge. Without alternative options, parents usually raise the children the way they were raised—for better or worse. Parenting is the toughest job in the world. Few of us are automatically equipped to handle it, nor are we given the tools when we first need them. Couples can learn the proper regimen for giving birth, but they learn little about what to do with the child once it is born. They then fall back on their own family or cultural experiences as their only reference point. It's a well-known fact that most people who were abused as children continue that cycle when they become parents. That's why having access to other options and the skill to use them is so critical to being a peaceful parent.

The second primary cause of child abuse is the parent's inability to manage anger. Abuse of any kind—physical, verbal, emotional—usually occurs in a fit of rage. By learning how to control and channel their anger, parents can usually avoid taking it out on their children.

Assuming you are already a peaceful parent and might want to train others, here are some basic questions you might ask:

1. **What does it take to be a trainer?**
   The fact is, almost anyone can do it. All you need is the information, experience in using it, and a desire to share it with others—along with, of course, a commitment to raising children peacefully.

2. **How much time will it take?**
   We have done everything we could to make peaceful parenting easy to learn and teach. We condensed the main book to a smaller size and laid out the seven habits and training steps in a concise, easy-to-read form. However, *peaceful parenting takes and deserves time.*

3. Where will I find others to train?

Parent support groups are one excellent source. Schools, churches, and social service agencies can also help find parents and caregivers and set up sessions. Urging friends and relatives to learn what you know is another way.

4. Can I learn to be a trainer?

You don't need to be a professional teacher or polished facilitator to convey your knowledge to others. The steps are easy. All it takes is a willingness to learn and teach.

5. Why should I do this? What is my motivation for training others? After all, I'm a peaceful parent and that takes enough time and patience. Why should I care what other parents do with their kids?

One possible result of this parent training will be that some of the participants will form support groups among themselves. Many parents we have worked with have shown a desire to discuss their child-rearing issues with others. More often than not, solutions to these concerns arise out of interchange within the group, rather that just from the facilitator. But once the session is over, the support network often breaks down. Wouldn't it be nice if that support could continue, if the group could continue to meet on its own and bring in new faces as well? The last section of this manual offers assistance on how to form and maintain parent support groups.

Peaceful parenting can't be done in a vacuum. To be effective, it has to permeate the culture. In this past century, we have all seen how pervasive violence can impact each and every one of us. A peaceful society can do the same. As we say, "Peace on earth begins at home." Each of our children has to grow up in the world to come. Don't we owe it to ourselves as parents and citizens to help that world be a peaceful one?

How to Use This Manual

*O*ur training program is designed to assist a wide range of caregivers, both men and women, develop peaceful parenting skills. We intended this curriculum to provide instruction in a group setting, but it can also be used on an individual basis. Peaceful parenting not only teaches families how to pursue harmony in the home, it helps them see and experience the choices they have every day to create even more peace within their family. Facilitators encourage parents to expand their views, experiences, and goals to include cooperation and peace and to integrate peaceful parenting into regular family life.

The program is designed to help parents become aware of the critical relationship between their communication skills with their children and overall family peace and harmony. Furthermore, they will realize that their own attitudes and skills can have profound influences not only on their children's self-esteem but also on their own self-worth. In the program, parents and caregivers learn about the connection between their methods of communication and interaction with each other and with their children, and the fulfillment of the basic emotional needs of belonging, security, and value. In the process, peaceful parenting helps parents realize that becoming effective problem solvers is a critical step in enhancing the self-worth and self-confidence of all family members.

Our program can help parents of infants and toddlers as well as parents of adolescents. It can also be used with high school students who are learning to be future parents.

To best use the child development and child management techniques in this manual, participants need to learn a variety of skills or habits. Among the most important are the following:

- **Managing your emotions.** Extremely angry parents often discipline excessively and destructively. Handling anger prudently improves discipline methods and creates a positive bond between parent and child.

- **Resolving conflicts peacefully.** Increasing their nonviolent problem-solving and discipline strategies gives parents many advantages in peacefully parenting their children.

- **Parenting your own way.** Each family is unique. Each parent and each child have individual personalities. Different strategies work better for certain children than for others. Parents need to learn that one size does not fit all.

- **Communicating openly.** By learning to communicate compassionately and empathically with their children, parents can improve relationships and decrease the need for corrective consequences.

- **Nurturing your child's self-esteem.** Positive approaches that enhance children's self-esteem, values, attitudes, and affection are very affirming.

- **Spending quality time with your children.** In general, the stronger the quality of the parent-child relationship, the smaller the amount of coercion a parent must use to obtain compliance and cooperation.

- **Disciplining in a consistent manner.** Children learn through the consequences of their actions. When consequences consistently follow their actions, they learn much more quickly.

How to Obtain These Habits

Caring parents acquire peaceful parenting habits in a variety of ways. Some find that reading relevant literature will be sufficient. Others benefit mostly through group endeavors like classes or workshops. Still others might learn on their own through individual home visits. Likewise, informal dialogue with friends and neighbors can help improve skills for some. For many parents, a combination of these experiences will enhance their acquisition. Regardless, it's important to acquire these habits as soon as possible in the parenting venture, preferably before any children are born.

How to Use This Manual

We wrote this manual to help parents become more effective, peaceful role models for their children. It does not convey a brand-new method or rationale for child rearing. Rather, it is the result of efforts to bring together knowledge about effective and well-established parenting strategies. Its underlying philosophy is that there is no one size that fits all. Instead, there are different strokes for different folks.

The manual can be used in its entirety in a step-by-step fashion. It can also be used in a more individualized, spontaneous manner. For example, a family may need to enhance only one skill because other skills are well in place.

Each habit-building session contains a purpose or goal, examples of the specific habit, and suggestions for activities that will help parents master that habit. Likewise, each session also contains guidelines for facilitators. These guidelines discuss how the new material can be presented in an informal, flexible fashion. Generally, emphasis is less on lecturing and more on interactive exchanges. Facilitators are also taught to be sensitive to nonverbal cues.

Parents who are uncomfortable with parts of the program may resist by challenging, questioning, or objecting. At times they may not follow through on their homework assignments. Facilitators must be aware of such patterns and find ways to help the parents become more open and less reluctant. Role-playing usually helps break down this resistance. A role-playing scenario will often involve three people: a parent, a child, and a coach.

General Guidelines: Setting up a Session

Mail a promotional flyer to potential referral sources well in advance. (See Handout 1, page 60.) At the initial session, involve parents as much as possible in all stages of planning. This includes what time to meet, where to meet, what to have as snacks, and perhaps how parents can take turns being cofacilitators.

Obtaining transportation and baby-sitting services is essential. Reminder calls can also be helpful. Make sure there is a comfortable room for the session, with a warm, supportive atmosphere. As much as possible, personalize and individualize each meeting to meet the needs of the group. Establish rapport by making sure the facilitator knows the names of the parents and what their goals are. Be sure to schedule time for a break and refreshments. Question and answer opportunities are also essential. At the beginning of each session, review and evaluate the previous week's skill. Facilitators should determine if parents had any problems implementing the strategies and skills. If so, some fine-tuning may need to occur. When these formal sessions are over, parents may want to arrange ongoing informal meetings on their own.

Individual Session Description

We designed each session to be about one and a half to two hours in length. There are seven formal sessions, but more can be added according to the needs of the group. Each session highlights one of the habits of peaceful parents. The first fifteen to thirty minutes of the session focus on reviewing and evaluating the home practice experiences from the previous session. The next forty-five minutes or so are devoted to the new topic or skill. After that, it may be helpful to take a break. At the end of the session, discuss the new topic for the next week in terms of the relevancy for each parent and homework assignments.

The review portion of the session gives facilitators an opportunity to see how well the parents are doing in mastering the new skills and ideas, and if there is any resistance. Individual home experiences should be shared with the entire group. Sharing can help melt resistance in certain individuals. When introducing the new content, try to tie it into comments or questions the parents made earlier in their review session.

To further lower resistance, point out to the parents how the skills being discussed may eventually help their children become happier, better adjusted, and more successful in the future.

Overall, we suggest that the maximum number of people in each session be around ten. This allows participants the opportunity to talk with each other and receive support from members of the group. It also keeps any one person from slipping into the background and not being an active participant. Having the group participants sit in a circle rather than in straight rows may facilitate interpersonal dialogue and help build a sense of rapport and community.

[handwritten margin notes:]

3 Goals
- *Tools*
- *How are are actions received / perceived?*
- *Sounding board - peer group.*

→ what exercises will we use? lists, role play, "bowl" technique, diaries,

Facilitator Characteristics

Peaceful parenting facilitators need to have certain prerequisites, qualifications, and characteristics. First of all, they must be committed to peaceful approaches to parenting and must value peacemaking in all aspects of our interconnected, interdependent, and interpersonal world.

Second, they need to have some basic understanding of child development and general psychology. Facilitators do not need to be professionals in the formal sense of the word. They need to have common sense, however, and a good understanding of how people change.

Additionally, facilitators need to understand and respect the parents' values and actions in dealing with their children. Our underlying belief is that parents are trying to do a good job and are doing the best they can. As a result of life's challenges and of some difficult behavioral problems, this is not always easy and their efforts are not always perfect. Facilitators need to acknowledge and value the parents' efforts. The facilitator is not a preacher who is trying to convert the parents to a different way of thinking. Ultimately, parents need to make the decisions for themselves while the facilitator presents all alternatives in a friendly, supportive manner.

Finally, facilitators need to have basic interpersonal skills that will help them develop rapport with parents. These skills include the capacity to understand and accurately reflect parental communication and interact respectfully and courteously with parents. The facilitators' style of interacting with the parents should be open and democratic and should reflect a positive self-concept. All in all, facilitators need to be models of good and appropriate communication for the parents.

Adapting the Peaceful Parenting Program to Special Families

Single Families

Single-parent families result from a number of factors including death, divorce, desertion, unplanned pregnancy. Although the vast majority of single-parent families are led by mothers, increasingly larger numbers live with fathers. Single parents, especially those not hampered by poverty, often raise children who are as happy and as productive as children from two-parent families. But many single parents are emotionally overstressed because of anger, loss, custody battles, or simply too many responsibilities, all of which increase the chances of child abuse. Single parents, especially, need to learn how to take advantage of networking, formal social services, informal social support, and their extended families. Single-parent families are usually much more financially strapped than two-parent families, and part of intervention may involve pursuing alternative sources of aid, both financial and otherwise. Facilitators of single-parent groups need to be especially sensitive to the special nature of those families.

Blended Families

Blended families are on the rise, since most adults who divorce will remarry and the children will become members of a new family unit.

The process of forming the new family, in and of itself, is stressful. However, there is even a greater amount of preexisting stress due to the separation that resulted in the formation of the single-parent family. Adults and children alike may be experiencing anger, guilt, loss, and fear. Just when the emotional turbulence of the event is subsiding, additional turmoil will occur within the combined family. Names, schools, jobs, and neighborhood friendships may change. In the face of such change, parents need help in keeping things as stable as possible, including school, baby-sitters, and schedules. They also need to learn new negotiating skills to minimize adjustment pains in the combined family. And they need to realize that the turmoil, anger, and confusion that emerge as the new family forms are quite normal. The outcome will be new rules, new relationships, and the emergence of the stepparent as an adult who is in charge and is a resource but who is not going to take the place of the biological parent. Children, in turn, will have to deal with loss of the past family, loss of fantasies, and loss of unrealistic expectations. These families need guidance and positive feedback in developing new problem-solving and conflict-resolution skills.

Adoptive Families

Many children in the United States are adopted, and many of them were in foster families before adoption. Children are placed for adoption for a variety of reasons including neglect, abuse, poverty, and inability to parent. Many adoptees are also from foreign countries. Adopted children are often at increased risk for developmental problems. Some were born prematurely. Many were born to very young, immature, and impulsive parents. Adoptive children have waves of intense emotion related to feelings of abandonment, betrayal, and rejection. Adoptive parents go through similar cycles of anger, inadequacy, and fear.

Each adoptive family is unique, and the peaceful parenting facilitator needs to be familiar with their individual characteristics. Pay attention as well to cultural, developmental, and special needs issues.

On the whole, the peaceful parenting facilitator ought to challenge any personal biases he or she has regarding alternative families. By respecting the values of these families, the facilitator can become a true helper.

Building Group Identity

In the first session, the facilitator creates a sense of group identity and resolves basic administrative or housekeeping tasks. When group members feel accepted and safe, they will be more inclined to share their personal experiences and put good effort into acquiring and practicing new skills. Group members need to establish rapport with each other, and with the facilitator. As these parents learn to trust one another and the facilitator, they will become more open and less defensive. Facilitators can help this process by displaying an easygoing style, sharing their personal experiences, and accepting parents without judgment or criticism. Also, facilitators must remember that parents do not deliberately try to hurt their children. They use the best parenting resources they have, which at times can be extremely limited.

As mentioned before, the ideal group size for these sessions is about ten parents. Seating works best in a circle or in a horseshoe shape, rather than in individual rows. Sitting around a large table affords a sense of security and comfort, and allows participants to have refreshments and take notes.

Facilitators will be more effective if they participate in the process as leaders, not as lecturers. They can share their views on parenting skills, styles, and knowledge validated through their own experience. This kind of active process motivates parents to be active rather than passive participants. It also helps develop trust within the group, which should eventually promote the openness and risk taking in role-playing exercises that help parents acquire new skills and attitudes.

Here are some suggested exercises to help establish cohesion and identify goals for each group member:

1. What's Your Name?
In this name accumulation game, one person starts out by saying, "Hi, my name is Jane." The next person says, "Hi, Jane. My name is Beth." The person next to Beth says, "Hi, Jane, Hi, Beth. My name is Joe." This continues until the last member of the circle addresses each previous person by name and then says his or her name. This is a fun and easy way for participants to get to know each other.

2. How Do You Feel?
This exercise focuses on individual feelings of uneasiness, discomfort, and unfamiliarity in the group setting. All members write down one thing that bothers, concerns, or distresses them about being in the group. The pieces of paper are folded in half and put in a bowl. Then, one at a time, members draw a slip, read the concern, and discuss it as if it were their own. If they draw their own piece of paper, they put it back in the bowl and pick again. Other group members are urged to comment about how they would feel if this were their concern. At the end, the facilitator destroys all the slips of paper.

3. When I Was a Child
In this activity, participants write down both a happy and an unhappy event from their own childhood. They fold their papers, put them in a bowl, and then draw them out, picking again if they receive their own. As members read other people's experiences, they are asked to comment about what the child was thinking or feeling. This helps them experience the event through the perspective of that child. Again, the facilitator destroys all the pieces of paper when the activity is over.

4. What My Child Does
This time, parents write down their child's bothersome behaviors. Again, they fold the pieces of paper and put them into a bowl. The parent who draws a card then discusses why that behavior might be problematic. Again, if parents pick their own, they should put it back and draw another one. Other group members are asked to comment and discuss their reactions. All pieces of paper are destroyed at the end.

5. Telling Your Story

Each parent talks about one problematic childhood behavior at home and identifies how much progress has been made in dealing with the problem. Using a scale from 1 to 10, where "1" is the problem being totally out of hand and "10" is the problem being completely solved, the parent is asked to come up with a number that identifies how problematic that behavior is right now. Then he or she is asked to pick one number higher and tell how things would be different at that number. For example, if the parent decides that the problem is now at a 4, one number higher would be 5. Now ask the parent to identify what would be different, how things would be better, and how they would know they were at a 5 instead of a 4. This should be written down so it can become a concrete goal for parents to work toward during the peaceful parenting training session.

Summary of Group-Building Exercises

1. Name accumulation: One person begins by saying, "Hi, my name is _____." The person next to them says, "Hi _____, my name is _____." This continues until the last person in the group addresses each of the previous members by name and then says his or her own name.

2. Members write down one thing that bothers them or concerns them about being in the group. The pieces of paper are folded in half and put into a bowl. One at a time, members draw a slip, read the concern, and discuss it as if it were their own. If they draw their own, they put it back and draw another.

3. Same as exercise 2, except members write down a happy and an unhappy event from their childhood.

4. Same as exercise 2, except members write down an upsetting or bothersome behavior their child engages in.

5. Members identify a problematic behavior, put it on a scale, and then come up with a modest goal in terms of behavioral change.

The Nuts and Bolts of Preparation

Getting a Sponsor

If you're a facilitator already working for a social service agency, you have a ready-made group of parents to work with. If not, try contacting a PTA, PTO, or early childhood facility. Churches may also be supportive of parenting groups.

Getting Parents to Sign up

Once a sponsor has been identified, talk to the leaders or the agency directors about how to get members to sign up. You should have a pamphlet ready to distribute.

Obtaining Space

Quite often, churches, schools, and agencies will donate space for affiliated groups. Libraries may donate space as well. If you are going to charge a fee, you may need to lease space at a nominal fee.

Display Table

You might set up a display table for the participants, with pamphlets, brochures, resource lists, and copies of *Peaceful Parenting in a Violent World* or *The Peaceful Parenting Handbook*.

Facilitator Attitudes

While you are examining the manual, consider your own attitude about parenting. You must also be willing to reach out and seek further information if you feel that your attitude might perhaps be a barrier to dealing effectively with parents using a nonviolent format.

Fees

Peaceful parenting was not designed as a money-making training program. However, there are expenses. Your time is important, and it is also important to pay for supplies. As a result, you may charge a nominal fee. High-risk families may not be able to afford a fee. However, we hope that no one will be turned away because of a lack of funds.

Registration Forms

Ask prospective members to fill out a registration form in advance, so that trainers can have some idea of the group composition and prepare accordingly. If, for example, there is an abundance of single parents, the training could be oriented accordingly.

Preparatory Reading

Read either *Peaceful Parenting in a Violent World* and/or *The Peaceful Parenting Handbook*. You don't need to be an expert, but you should be informed about current topics, approaches, and strategies in dealing with parenting issues. We also encourage facilitators to read a variety of other books. Here are a few examples:

Allen, Juliet. *What Do I Do When ...?* San Luis Obispo, Calif.: Impact Publishers, 1983.

Barkley, Russell A. *Defiant Children.* New York: Guilford Publications, Inc., 1997.

Clabby, John F., and Maurice J. Elias. *Teach Your Child Decision Making.* Garden City, New York: Doubleday & Company, Inc., 1987.

Farber, Adele, and Elaine Maglish. *Siblings Without Rivalry.* New York: Avon Books, 1987.

Phelan, Thomas W. *1-2-3 Magic.* Glen Ellyn, Ill.: Child Management, Inc.,1985.

Sloane, Howard N. *The Good Kid Book.* Champaign, Ill.: Research Press, 1988.

Turecki, Stanley. *The Difficult Child.* New York: Bantam Books, 1985.

Audiovisual Aids

It may be helpful to have some of the following equipment:

- A blackboard or newsprint on which to record ideas

- Handouts for parents

- An overhead projector to highlight some of the material like the goals for each meeting and the key ideas

- A sign-up sheet for those who attend

Managing the Group Effectively

Each facilitator has a unique style for working with groups. Many of you have not made a career out of leading groups. There are some pointers that will maximize everyone's effectiveness and contribution, thus contributing to the success of your groups.

It's a good idea to write the goals in large print on either the chalkboard, newsprint, or a transparency. During the course of the meeting, if the group gets off task, it's easy to use the visual representation to get back on track. Also, frequent reference to the goals helps members remember them.

To keep a large group on track is quite challenging. When you think the group is getting off track, a number of strategies can get them back in focus. You might say, "That's really an interesting subject and we could talk about it for hours, but I'm afraid if we do that, we won't meet our goals." Or you could try, "That's a really pertinent topic. Since we have limited time for discussion right now, I suggest we pursue it either at the next meeting or after today's meeting for those who are interested." All in all, continue to refer back to the list of goals that are visually evident.

Allowing the group members to express their own thoughts and feelings is very important. This encourages group participation. It's very important that no group ideas be criticized or demeaned. You, and other group members, need to handle disagreements in a tactful fashion. Disagreement should be viewed as another opinion, not as a statement of fact.

As group facilitators, it is important to explore and understand a person's point of view before expressing agreement or disagreement. Group members need to feel that facilitators understand fully what they are saying.

If there are some brainstorming sessions, it may be helpful to have a volunteer write the ideas on the chalkboard or the newsprint. The use of newsprint allows you to retain the ideas for subsequent meetings if necessary.

When it's time to end the meeting, it is important to identify when the next meeting will be and what the purpose will be.

Graduation

Upon completion of the training program, we recommend participants be given an official certificate. They should be congratulated and encouraged to continue with a parent support group or additional parent training as necessary.

Ordering Books

Books can be ordered easily by contacting any bookstore or the publisher at:

Resource Publications, Inc.
160 E. Virginia St. #290
San Jose, CA 95112
(888) 273-7782

Website

Trainers can receive updated information on a regular basis by accessing the Peaceful Parenting website (www.peacefulparenting.org).

Handouts

This book contains twenty-six handouts in the Appendix. These should be photocopied for participants. Each week, give the parents only the handouts they need for that session. Otherwise they may feel overwhelmed.

Part Two

The Seven Habits
Of Peaceful Parents

Habit 1

Managing Your Emotions

Purpose

The purpose of this session is to understand the dynamics of anger as a function of frustration, pain, fear, discouragement, guilt, and grief; to identify twisted thinking that leads to excessive anger outbursts; and to acquire at least five new skills for dealing with anger.

What Parents Will Learn

1. To recognize and identify negative thoughts that lead to destructive anger

2. To identify the emotional dynamics behind anger

3. To express their anger in a less destructive way

Background for the Facilitator: Understanding Emotions

When people become angry, they often say or do things they later regret. In fits of anger, parents may spank a child, call a child "stupid," or give their spouse the silent treatment. Intense angry feelings can lead to unproductive, sometimes destructive actions.

When we think about angry situations, we realize that how we perceive a situation often influences what our emotional reaction is going to be. Our beliefs or thoughts affect how we are going to feel. What we tell ourselves about a situation truly determines how we are going to react. If we have negative interpretations or beliefs about situations, our emotions tend to be intense and lead to ineffective, self-defeating behaviors. By changing how we think about a situation, we can actually alter our emotional reaction to it and ultimately change our actions.

In summary, when we look at understanding our emotions, we notice that first some event, situation, or problem occurs. We make a silent statement about that situation based on our beliefs, attitudes, or opinions. The statement we make in our heads can be realistic or unrealistic, accurate or twisted. Then, we experience consequences: our feelings first, and then our actual actions. If our self-statements are accurate and rational, our feelings tend to be well controlled and our actions are effective. If our self-statements are irrational or twisted, our feelings can be exaggerated and overly intense, and our actions ineffective and self-defeating. We often cannot change events or situations. However, we can change the way in which we respond to them.

- Beliefs influence feelings and actions.

- A change in attitude can create a change in action.

- Our interpretations of situations, not the situations themselves, lead to anger.

- To a large extent, we choose how intensely we react to an unfortunate situation.

Session Plan

The first session focuses on dealing with negative emotions, especially anger. There are three exercises, and the total session should take approximately sixty to seventy-five minutes. The goals of this session are to help parents understand some of the other feelings that tend to be behind anger, identify negative thoughts that lead to anger, and learn to express their anger in a healthier way.

On a 1 to 10 scale, ask parents to determine how effectively they handle their anger toward their children at the present time. A 1 would mean handling anger in an extremely destructive, verbally violent fashion. A 10 would mean handling anger in a constructive, educational, beneficial way that communicates messages clearly yet preserves the child's self-esteem and minimizes the child's defensiveness. Ask parents to make a note of what their rating is, because at the end of the program, they will compare their ratings on the first day of the workshop with those at the end.

■ Exercise 1:
Identifying the Primary Feelings

By way of introduction, ask parents, "How many of you had some angry feelings today?" Have the parents look at the events that seemed to lead up to the anger, and then ask them, "What were you concerned with?" "What were you worried about?" or "What were you afraid of?" Initially most parents are taken aback by those questions. However, the answers underscore the dynamics of anger. Anger is a secondary feeling. It is usually a manifestation of a primary feeling. Fear is the most common primary feeling underlying anger. Other underlying feelings include guilt, loss, and grief. Sometimes pain, frustration, and discouragement are also contributing feelings.

As an example, ask parents how they react when their toddler darts into the street or sticks a paper clip into an electrical outlet. Most parents will describe how they were very angry, yelled at the child, perhaps jerked the child, and dispensed some corporal punishment. However, when asked what they were afraid of, parents will usually say, "I thought he might die." This is a graphic example that most parents can identify with. It helps them understand that fear is often the feeling behind anger. It might be fear of ridicule, fear of embarrassment, fear of disapproval, or some other fear. It also can be related to a sense of guilt. Parents may recall that when they confront a child misbehaving, the child is often angry. Most likely, the child is also feeling guilt because the parents have expressed some disapproval. The guilt, however, is initially translated into anger. Many parents may also experience the loss of a dream or a hope when they realize that their child, for one reason or another, will not live up to their dreams and expectations.

Accordingly, when parents feel angry with a child, advise them to ask themselves, "What am I afraid of?" rather than, "What am I angry about?" The answer to this simple question can often help them better understand the dynamics of anger.

To begin the exercise, ask the parents to team up with another person who is not their spouse or partner. Then in a four- or five-minute activity, ask each parent to identify a situation involving their children in which they became angry. Next ask them to identify the primary feeling behind the anger. They might use leading questions such as "What was I afraid of?", "What did I lose?" or "What did I feel guilty about?" After each parent has had an opportunity to explore primary feelings, discuss everyone's reactions to the exercise and ask whether group members are beginning to get a different perspective on anger.

■ Exercise 2:
Identifying Unrealistic Thoughts That Lead to Negative Actions

Most of the time, unrealistic and irrational self-statements are identified by certain words. One of the most common is the word *should*. Other red-flag words include *always, never, hate, can't stand, every, never, all, nothing*. Also, any name calling in a self-statement is likely to be twisted.

As an example, Jane just finished washing her white kitchen floor. Her daughter opened the door and let the dogs run through with their muddy paws. That is the situation. Jane could make a variety of self-statements about that situation. On one extreme, she could say or just think, "What a mess! I can't stand it! I work all day and what thanks do I get? Everybody is inconsiderate and they don't give a darn about anything I do!" With this set of self-statements, Jane may scream at her child, throw towels, and stomp around. On the other hand, she could say, "Darn it. I should have told her not to come in. Oh well, it could be worse. It will just take a few minutes to clean up the footprints. Next time I will make sure that the dogs are in the house and won't be coming through." Obviously, the response in this case would be quite different.

In another example, Jim tells his father, "I hate you. You're just mean and I can't stand you." At the one extreme, the father could say, "He doesn't love me. Look at all I've done for him and he shows no appreciation. I can't stand not being treated with respect. I'll show him who's boss." Subsequent actions might include slapping, yelling, or worse. On the other hand, the father could say, "Boy, it's obvious that Jim is really angry and upset with me. Something must have happened for him to feel so bad. I don't like what he said, but I also realize this may be the only way he feels he can get any attention. We need to discuss this when he is calmer." Again, in this situation, the response would be peaceful and likely effective.

In approaching anger this way, we are not trying to minimize or avoid negative feelings. But many of those feelings are overreactions based on unrealistic and twisted thoughts, which can result in nonproductive behaviors and negatively influence the parent-child relationship. With the peaceful parenting model, parents have some choice in terms of how they react to a situation. It's erroneous for a parent to say, "He made me mad." Although the child did something provocative, the parent should say, "I exaggerated the situation and made it worse than it is by overreacting."

This model does not excuse the child's behavior. Instead, it focuses on the parents dealing with the behavior in a reasonable, self-controlled manner, so they can be more effective in their child rearing.

Keep in mind that we are not born with self-statements or beliefs. We acquire them through experience. Most of the time we learn them from our parents, but we also learn from other influential people including teachers, ministers, coaches, and other relatives and friends. As with most things, self-statements become more deeply ingrained over time and with practice.

To begin the exercise, give parents Handout 2 (page 61), which contains some unrealistic self-statements about child rearing that could result in ineffective and self-defeating actions, and some more realistic self-statements about parenting. Ask parents to identify the fallacies or the inconsistencies or the illogical reasoning in the twelve unrealistic statements.

Next, ask parents to chart the self-statements that are related to anger for a week, using the Cognitive Diary handout (Handout 3, page 62) for this purpose. They should keep a journal for at least a week about anger outbursts, identifying situations that result in angry responses on their part. Then, they should stop, step back, think about, and write down what self-statement preceded the anger and the ineffective action. Ask them to look for key words such as *should, all, nothing, never, everyone, nobody, hate, can't stand*. Next, they should come up with a more realistic, rational, sensible self-statement and write it down—even though they may not fully identify with it or believe it at the time. Trying on new self-statements is like trying on a new pair of shoes. At first, they feel somewhat stiff and unbending, perhaps slightly uncomfortable. With time, however, they become more comfortable and seem to fit much better.

In addition to identifying and changing the self-statements, ask parents to identify the events, the buttons, or the triggers that often cause parental stress. We can take preventive action and decrease, possibly even eliminate the likelihood of certain events happening. For example, if two children start bickering whenever they sit next to each other in the back seat of the car, it may be possible to change the seating arrangement or to have activities for each of them to do separately. At the dinner table, if one particular seating arrangement seems to lead to more conflict, then changing the seating arrangement could work. Sometimes, especially in stressful situations like mealtime, children may need to eat in shifts to avoid bickering. If homework after dinner is always a hassle, perhaps doing it earlier would prevent that stress. In any event, the cognitive diary can help identify those events that might be avoided by some preventive strategies.

■ Exercise 3:
Now I Know My ABCs

In addition to changing self-statements and decreasing the likelihood of trigger events, other anger management strategies can be helpful. This program includes a list of twenty-six different solutions, based on each letter of the alphabet, which can contribute to peaceful and effective anger management (Handout 4, page 63).

Ask parents to review these strategies and pick at least five that they think will be meaningful and feasible for them. Then, if time permits, have a role-play activity to allow parents to begin to practice some of the ideas. There is some partial overlap with the cognitive or self-statement approach to anger management. For the most part, however, the twenty-six strategies are above and beyond the cognitive approach. Ideally, role-playing will involve three members: the parent, the child, and a coach. The first time, ask the parent to show what poorly managed angry responses look like. Then they can practice the alternatives until they become comfortable with them.

Conclusion

Anger is an important feeling. It energizes us, motivates us, and encourages us to be assertive. Anger is a very natural feeling that we all experience. It can, however, be harmful. It is physically harmful when we hurt others (kick, hit, or throw). It's emotionally abusive when we put others down or hurt their feelings. Anger can damage relationships because it blocks communication and fosters isolation. We can also hurt ourselves when our anger causes headaches, stomachaches, or ulcers, and when we harbor feelings of guilt, sadness, and depression. Repressed anger can result in substance abuse, major health problems, violence, or eating disorders.

To help motivate parents to deal assertively and effectively with their own parental anger, it's important to have them recognize the negative outcomes of poorly managed anger. These include yelling, name calling, swearing, corporal punishment, abuse, trauma for the children, guilt for the parents, or lowered self-esteem for all. On the other hand, there are many positive outcomes of well-managed parental anger, including better communication, true changes in children's behavior, enhanced self-esteem for all, and a peaceful family atmosphere. Ask the group members for concrete examples of both negative and positive outcomes of parental anger. Highlighting the different types of outcomes can truly motivate parents to make lasting changes.

For the next session, ask parents to complete the cognitive diary and bring it back. They are to pay special attention to the cognitive dimension of the diary. Also ask them to report on how they have used their five new anger management techniques with their children, spouses, or anybody else during the week.

Tips for Facilitators

When discussing the cognitive diaries:

- Give as many examples as possible.

- Have parents offer their own interpretation of the twenty-six anger management solutions when possible.

- Be sure to have parents role-play their five selected strategies if time permits.

- Work in groups of three so that everybody gets a chance to practice.

Materials Needed

- Handout 2: Unrealistic Self-Statements and Realistic Self-Statements

- Handout 3: Cognitive Diary

- Handout 4: ABCs of Anger Management

Habit 2

Resolving Conflicts Peacefully

Purpose

The purpose of this session is to help parents realize that most peaceful solutions will work, when implemented properly.

In addition, parents will come to realize that not all family problems belong to them. In some cases the children need to solve their own problems.

What Parents Will Learn

1. To implement the basic components of peaceful behavioral strategies (e.g., ignoring, positive and corrective feedback, contracts, Grandma's rule, logical and natural consequences)—change occurs in small steps

2. To construct behavioral charts to evaluate their programs and determine which solutions are effective, and to accurately identify the types of reinforcers that will work for their children

3. To identity which behavioral strategies are especially effective for initiating change, and which specific incentives will continue to maintain ongoing behavioral change

Background for the Facilitator: Peaceful Alternative Solutions

Give specific examples of how families have used alternative solutions for sticky problems. For example, you can point out how a variety of solutions can be used to increase compliance, minding, and cooperation.

Peaceful and creative problem-solving in families encompasses child discipline, but also self-discipline for both parents and children. Discipline focuses on teaching children the skills to help them function effectively in the social world when they grow up. Throughout, it's important to assess the impact of a particular disciplinary style on the child's self-esteem. Discipline affects not only behavior but also values and beliefs. Moderate rather than extreme forms of discipline tend to be most effective. Overly permissive or authoritarian parents are usually ineffective. Extreme permissiveness or extreme authoritarianism can damage a child's self-esteem and result in a variety of behavioral and emotional problems.

When it comes to problem-solving, reflective listening and "I" message communication are helpful but not necessarily sufficient. Using these important communication skills can help establish an atmosphere in which additional strategies and solutions may be generated and readily agreed on.

Behavioral strategies are often among the most effective and readily implemented solutions and interventions. Some of the important ingredients of behavioral modification are discussed in *The Peaceful Parenting Handbook*.

In summary, remember that we learn by watching others and from the consequences of our behavior; and that behavioral changes often occur in small steps. Essentially, there are three types of consequences that help shape behavior: ignoring (which usually decreases a behavior), positive consequences (which usually increase a behavior), and negative consequences or corrective feedback (which usually decrease or stop the behavior).

- Empathic communication helps establish an atmosphere for effective discipline.

- We learn by watching others.

- We learn from the consequences of our behavior.

- Behavioral changes often occur in small increments.

■ Exercise 1:
Learning about Behavioral Interventions

Give participants Handout 5 (page 64), which contains summaries of eleven different types of peaceful/behavioral interventions. Whenever possible, the eleven interventions can be role-played using triads. Try to avoid having spouses participate in the same triad. This strategy avoids the introduction of other issues and provides a better learning opportunity overall.

1. Brainstorming
Brainstorming is a creative way of generating solutions to problems. It can occur in a family meeting or with the parents alone. List as many solutions to a problem as family members can generate. No idea is unacceptable during the initial generation stage. Then through a sorting process, either weed out or reconsider the solutions. At some point, complete the ranking and implement the most likely solution. Give a family solution two to four weeks of consistent implementation before deciding whether or not it is effective.

2. Contracts
Contracts can be especially effective with adolescents. Contracts are written agreements in which the parties specify directly which behaviors they agree to do. Usually, contracts consist of positive statements that specify what the parents will do and also what the children will do. They are signed by family members and there can be a date for renegotiation or assessment. Contracts are often effective because they are a functional form of communication that respects the roles of various family members and addresses the specific needs of a family. They are also a model for negotiating problems and agreements in the future.

3. Time-Outs/Groundings

Groundings are essentially a form of time-out. "Time-out" literally means a time away from pleasurable activities and experiences. With younger children, including those in middle childhood, it often consists of spending time alone in an isolated corner of the house, in a bathroom or perhaps a laundry room. A child's bedroom is not a good time-out place because it's too rewarding. Usually a child is placed in time-out for approximately one minute for each year of age. We recommend that a child be given one warning to either begin doing something the parent would like them to do or to stop doing something the parent dislikes. If the child doesn't comply after ten to fifteen seconds, the direction is repeated. If compliance doesn't occur within a few seconds after the second direction, the child is put in time-out. In some situations, such as hurting somebody else, there is no warning. Sometimes, especially with a noncompliant child, the directions may need to be given repeated times with each noncompliance resulting in the fixed time-out experience. With older children, time-out essentially becomes grounding. They may be grounded to their room, to the house, or to the yard. They may be grounded from telephone, television, some friends, or all friends. Usually we recommend that a grounding not be excessive in length but that the severity of the noncompliance determine the intensity of the grounding.

4. Positive Consequences/Rewards

Rewards are reinforcers that are typically pleasant or enjoyable experiences. They are consequences that encourage behavior.
It's important to remember that what is pleasurable or enjoyable for a child may or may not be for a parent. Effective reinforcers are truly rewarding for the child whose behavior needs to change. In terms of figuring out what is going to be rewarding for certain children, watch what they choose to do or to play with. Handout 6 (page 65) details a variety of positive consequences.

5. Corrective Consequences/Punishments

Corrective consequences or punishments are usually unpleasant and to be avoided. Their purpose is to decrease undesirable behavior. Corrective consequences can have very undesirable side effects because they can break down the parent-child relationship. Withholding rewards or reinforcers is usually the least damaging type of corrective consequence. Once again, determine the idea of unpleasantness from the child's point of view, not from the parent's. For example, a teacher might think that having a child sit in the hallway rather than stay in the classroom would be punishing. In fact, it may be rewarding for some children because they don't have to do the work in the classroom, and they can laugh, talk, and entertain other students in the hallway. A parent might think that taking a child on a fishing trip would be a reward, but if a child does not like fishing, it could be a punishment. Handout 6 (page 65) gives examples of corrective consequences.

6. Encouragement and Praise

Encouragement and praise are generally social reinforcers. They should be specific and concrete and should be spoken as soon as possible after the desired behavior occurs. See Tips for Terrific Talk (Handout 7, page 66).

7. The Role of Fines

Fines essentially involve a loss of reinforcement, which occurs after an undesired behavior. The fines usually occur in small amounts.
For example, a child might be fined five or fifteen minutes of TV time for a certain type of noncompliance. This is simply a loss of reward. Similarly, a child might have to go to bed ten, fifteen, or twenty minutes early for each minor transgression. Once again, the consequence is a loss of rewarding time. Fines are often beneficial for impulsive types of behavior such as cussing, unacceptable language, and name calling.

8. Grandma's Rule

Grandma's Rule is basic behavioral modification. It means that highly desired behaviors are contingent upon less desired behaviors. In other words, children have to do things they don't enjoy doing, so that they can enjoy things they do like to do. With Grandma's Rule two behaviors are involved: one the child thinks is important and one the parent thinks is important. The behavior the child believes is important comes after the behavior the parent believes is important. For example, Grandma perhaps used to say, "You can have dessert after you wash dishes." Another example would be, "As soon as you finish mowing the lawn, we can go to the movies."

9. Logical/ Natural Consequences

Natural consequences occur in a cause-and-effect fashion. For example, if you don't dress warmly, you will naturally be cold. If you don't get enough sleep, then you will be tired. Logical consequences involve something that may not occur automatically but nevertheless are reasonable consequences. For instance, if a child soils his pants, a logical consequence would be that he would clean his clothes himself and he would have to take a bath. Another example might involve children who fight over toys. A logical consequence would be that they would be separated for a while and that the toy they fought over would be put away.

10. Conflict Resolution

First, have both sides define the conflict or the problem as they see it. Write it down objectively without prejudice or judgment. Before there can be any resolution, there has to be an agreement as to what the problem or conflict is. Once the conflict has been identified, brainstorm all possible alternative solutions. Again, this should be wide-open with no judgments or prejudices. All members need to feel they are equal and that their solution will at least be considered. Once a wide variety of solutions have been proposed, each side will eliminate or cross out the solution or option they consider to be least acceptable. This process should leave at least one or two solutions that are not crossed out. If by chance all solutions are crossed out, agree to meet again and reprocess options. Once both sides have come to an agreement on a possible solution, they should identify specifically what their responsibilities are. These should also be written down. At that time, they should decide on a time when the solution will be evaluated for acceptance and effectiveness.

11. The Family Meeting

The family meeting is a time for sharing, discussing, deciding, and evaluating—an open forum in which all members can speak without interruption or fear of ridicule. It can also be a time for planning and having fun. The family meeting should occur in a comfortable place, perhaps at the dinner table or in the family room; it should be convenient and relaxed and at a time when nobody has immediate plans afterward. In families with older children, leadership can rotate so the children become familiar with leadership roles. Family members should take turns speaking and then listen when others talk. Focus on one item at a time. Also, post an agenda in advance, so family members have a chance to think about items to be discussed and to add to it. If there are some sensitive issues on the agenda, use conflict resolution strategies to help solve them.

Comments on Consequences

1. The Value of Predetermined Consequences

When parents are caught up in the emotion of discipline, they often overreact. Frequently, an angry parent will proclaim a punishment that is unrealistic, exaggerated, and excessive. For example, a parent might be in a bad mood and overreact to a mild transgression and shout out, "You're grounded for a month." Predetermined consequences prevent overreaction and excessive punishment, which is often later recanted. This inconsistency will teach children that parents' actions can't be predicted. There is also a resulting security issue, because children cannot count on their parents to follow through. Predetermined consequences are usually written down quite specifically so when noncompliance occurs, the parent and the child know immediately what the consequence is. As stated previously, the quality of the parent-child relationship is best preserved when punishments are delivered in a nonemotional, matter-of-fact manner.

2. Dealing with Unruly Children in Time-Out and Grounding

If young children refuse to go to time-out, escort them by the hand. If older children refuse, tell them that for every minute they delay in going to time-out, they will have to go to bed that much earlier or they will lose that much television time that day. If children make noise during the time-out, ignore it or add on extra time. It's important to be consistent in this regard. For younger children who run away, *restraint is appropriate*. Older children can again be told that they will lose other privileges, such as going to bed early or losing television time, if they don't comply with time-out.

3. The Characteristics of Effective Consequences

Administer consequences immediately after the behavior. Even a few minutes' delay affects their meaningfulness. As much as possible, the consequence should fit the behavior whether it is positive or negative.

This is not always easy, which is why time-outs and groundings are often used for corrective consequences and token systems are used for positive consequences.

■ Exercise 2: Charting Behaviors

To determine whether a solution is effective, parents need to record how frequently the behavior they want to change actually occurs before any intervention is implemented. Usually, a week of baseline is sufficient. Then, they should start the behavioral intervention and continue recording the behavior. This is to let parents know if the intervention is effective. Interventions need to be in place for three to four weeks before we can see whether the desired change occurs. If it occurs earlier, that's a bonus! Give the parents some behavior recording charts so they can chart a behavior at home (Handout 8, pages 67–68).

In the introductory part of the first session, parents were instructed to pick a target behavior at home that they would like to see changed. At this time, ask them to write the target behavior on the Behavior Recording Chart. Next, ask them to look at the eleven interventions to determine an intervention program that would be helpful in bringing about behavioral change.

For example, suppose Bob and Tammy state their goal is to improve their children's cooperation and listening. Bob and Tammy chose to use positive consequences for compliance and corrective consequences for not listening or noncompliance. They also decided to sharply increase the amount of encouragement and praise. Additionally, they used Grandma's Rule as a natural way of encouraging cooperation. Using the principle of predetermined consequences, Bob and Tammy carefully identified the rewards and the corrective consequences. Their program was written down to enhance the likelihood of follow-through and consistency. Have the parents review Handout 8 so they can see how consistency on the part of Bob and Tammy resulted in positive behavior change.

During the first week, Bob and Tammy gave many directions that resulted in a high rate of noncompliance, indicated by the second and third columns. Beginning on the eighth day, they coupled their directions with an intervention. While they did not have 100 percent follow-through (the difference between the numbers in columns 2 and 4), their consistency was sufficient to produce higher rates of compliance as shown in column 3.

Materials Needed

- Handout 5: Summery of Behavior Strategies
- Handout 6: Positive Consequences/Rewards and Corrective Consequences/Punishments
- Handout 7: Tips for Terrific Talk
- Handout 8: Behavior Recording Chart

Habit 3

Parenting Your Own Way

Purpose

The purpose of this session is to help parents realize that effective parenting solutions vary from family to family and even from child to child within a family—one size does not fit all families.

What Parents Will Learn

1. To discover insights into their own personalities

2. To understand their children's temperamental differences and developmental characteristics, and thus better understand the personalities of each child

3. How structural differences can affect child-parent relationships

4. To identify a number of other variables also affect the child-parent relationship

Background for the Facilitator: Different Strokes for Different Folks

Each family is unique. There is no one way for all families to grow and do things together. Parents have different personalities; therefore some parenting strategies work well for one kind of personality but not for another. Even within the same family, children have different personalities and temperaments. These diversities affect the quality of parenting. At different developmental stages, different types of discipline work better than others. Being cognizant of children's developmental stages is important for parents in terms of identifying appropriate goals and strategies. Additionally, many other factors influence effective parenting. These factors include health issues, religious differences, cultural diversity, and the actual composition of the family, whether it is a nuclear, blended, or single-parent family.

- Parents need to use discipline strategies that are compatible with their own personalities.

- As much as possible, disciplinary strategies should be consistent with children's temperaments.

- Behavioral strategies work better for young children, and cognitive, rational problem-solving strategies often work well with adolescents. Match the discipline to the developmental age.

- Blended families require generous amounts of time to establish boundaries and to form disciplinary roles.

- Health, ethnicity, religion, and socioeconomic status can have a significant effect on child-parent relationships.

Session Plan

In contrast to many parenting approaches and their orientations, peaceful parenting presumes that each family is unique, that there is no one approach or solution that is going to be effective all the time for all the children. As a result, peaceful parenting focuses on parents' understanding subtle differences and nuances in a variety of variables and using this knowledge to help establish the most effective and least restrictive disciplinary program for each child.

■ Exercise 1:
What Kind of a Parent Am I?

Parents can obtain insight into their own personalities in a number of ways. They can read psychology books about personality types and try to analyze themselves. They can consult a psychologist and arrange to take personality tests. Or they can look at their basic parenting style and develop insights. An example of this approach is discussed in *Parenting: Four Patterns of Child Rearing* by Samellyn Wood, Roger Bishop, and Davene Cohen (New York: Hart Publishing, 1978). The book discusses four different patterns of parenting, rating them all equally.

No particular pattern is recommended; the parenting styles are simply different. Our Parenting Styles handout (Handout 9, page 69) summarizes the four styles, called the Potter, the Gardener, the Maestro, and the Consultant. Urge parents to decide which one most closely fits their personality. This knowledge will provide insight into which parenting strategies will be most effective.

1. **The Potter:** Potters find it easy to be consistent and often use behavioral approaches. They maintain charts and checklists, and monitor the changes in their child's behavior. Also, they tend to be goal oriented.

2. **The Gardener:** Gardeners use preventive, distracting, and diversionary tactics. They believe primarily in positive feedback and rarely use corrective consequences. Overall, they are serious students of child development, and carefully factor in their child's developmental level in terms of expectations and consequences.

3. **The Maestro:** Maestros focus on self-esteem. They are also goal oriented. In general, they want to identify and maximize a child's area of strength. In their view, as long as a child's self-esteem is well nourished, the child will be responsible and achieve reasonably well.

4. **The Consultant:** Consultants are advisers who focus on problem-solving strategies. They see themselves as partnering with their children. Cognitive, rational problem solving and decision making are the ultimate goals in their parental philosophy.

Ask the participants to break into groups of two, making sure that they are not with spouses. Let them discuss the various attributes and characteristics of each of the four parenting types and begin to tentatively identify what sort of parent they are. Again, remind them that no one type is better than another and all are valid and appropriate. After the dyads have met for about five or ten minutes, hold a brief group discussion about what various parents have learned.

■ Exercise 2:
Determining Temperament

Facilitators help parents determine the personality characteristics of each of their children. Children aren't all born alike. Each child's personality is determined by a number of factors including heredity, the mother's physical and emotional health during pregnancy, events that occur during birth, and events that happen afterward. Even at birth, children show personality differences. Within the first few days, some children react to change with fear or apprehension, while others react with glee and joy. Some children respond quickly, while others are slower to react. Some seem to be placid, while still others show intense mood changes. Some are attentive while others are easily distracted.

Parents should be encouraged to study the Temperament handout (Handout 10, page 70) and determine differences among their children. Drs. Alexander Thomas and Stella Chess (*Temperament and Development* [New York: Brunner/Mazel, 1977]) have identified nine different factors that influence temperamental differences.

As much as possible, parents should make their discipline expectations consistent with the child's temperament. This is challenging, since there are often temperamental differences among children. Children may have the same gene pool, but different temperaments. Behavior problems often are nothing more than temperamental differences. Highly active children may be viewed as noncompliant and disobedient because they have trouble sitting still. Distractible children may be seen as lazy or unmotivated. Children who are slow to warm up may be described as anxious or insecure.

One strategy parents can use to deal with individual differences is to reframe or relabel their children's characteristics. Instead of being called "hyperactive," a child could be referred to as "vigorous," "energetic," or "vivacious." Instead of being described as "distractible and inattentive," a child could be considered "expansive," "inquisitive," and "independent." If parents have children with rather intense mood swings, remaining calm and even-tempered during the difficult moods can help children. Children who are slow to warm up need to be allowed to adapt to their surroundings gradually. Youngsters who are easily distracted or inattentive need both firmness and patience. Children's temperaments can significantly influence parental behavior. Adaptable, pleasant, and good-natured children can lead parents to believe they are adequate and confident parents. Difficult children often make parents feel inadequate. This can leave parents feeling so anxious and threatened, they may become abusive.

Parents should realize that, to a large extent, temperament is an enduring and persistent personality trait, although it can be modified to a certain extent through interaction with the environment. No matter how persistent and creative parents are, they most likely will not be able to make an overly active, distractible, inattentive child sit and concentrate for long periods. Just knowing they aren't responsible for temperament may help alleviate the crushing burden of guilt and anxiety that weighs on many parents who believe they have failed and may allow them to focus on changing some environmental factors.

Understanding temperament does not mean condoning all of its consequences. Parents can modify the results of temperament by altering consequences. Overly active children may need breaks, yet they can still be redirected to return to an activity later. Shy, withdrawn children can be encouraged to participate in gradual steps. Disruptive children can learn to express their frustrations in more acceptable ways.

Once again, it might be helpful to break into dyads and help parents begin to understand their children's temperament by figuring out where each child is on the various dimensions.

■ Exercise 3:
Determining Developmental Levels

The peaceful parenting program helps parents determine each child's developmental stage and the behavioral characteristics of that stage. Although all children go through the same sequence of developmental stages in the same order, they don't always do it in the same time frame. Some children are leapers and reach the various stages somewhat early. Others are creepers and obtain each phase more gradually. Parental frustration often results from inappropriate expectations. For example, many parents become upset when their six- and seven-year-olds don't seem to understand rational reasoning. The truth of the matter is that although psychologists used to believe the age of reason was about seven, they now realize it is closer to eleven or twelve. Children begin to develop some abstracting and concept formation skills around eight, but they don't actually begin to understand cause-and-effect reasoning as adults do until they are about eleven years old.

Help parents set reasonable developmental expectations for their children by helping them understand the Growth and Development handout (Handout 11, pages 71–72). This handout lists some of the important developmental aspects at different ages as they relate to discipline. Parents should not just look at the chronological age of their child. Instead, they should also consider the development stages just before and after their child's chronological age. Children don't go through all aspects of their developmental level at precisely the same time. With developmentally delayed children, for example, parents may need to look at even younger developmental levels. However, even very bright children do not necessarily show signs of maturation consistent with their intellectual ability.

Again in dyads, parents should consider the developmental stage of each of their children, remembering that the chronological age and the developmental age may not necessarily be the same.

■ Exercise 4:
Being Aware of Family Differences

Each family has a certain structure. Some are nuclear families with both parents. Others are stepfamilies or blended families. Some are single-parent families. Increasingly, there are families in which grandparents are raising their grandchildren. Each of these unique structures may very well require some special parental flexibility and modification. Stepparents, for example, need to build rapport carefully before they are in a position to act in a more authoritative role. If they prematurely act authoritatively and dogmatically, it can trigger childhood resentment and rebellion. Single-parent families often have few resources and supports, and need to establish disciplinary programs that require realistic levels of time and energy. Grandparents playing the role of parents need to guard against becoming permissive and indulgent.

In families with stepparents, discipline strategies need to be discussed before remarriage to make sure differences are resolved. In the beginning, the stepparent needs to develop rapport and become acquainted with the children, then he or she can gradually assume the disciplinary role. As a result, in the beginning, the biological parent may need to assume primary disciplinary responsibility. In time, the children will learn to respect and mind stepparents. In blended families, boundaries should be especially well defined. Family meetings are very beneficial in helping stepfamilies understand boundaries, expectations, and preferences. Many children find it difficult to openly love both their biological parent and their stepparent of the same gender. Stepparents need to understand that children may feel guilty if they have a good relationship with them. Power struggles are common among stepsiblings and need to be dealt with up-front and in a timely fashion.

A number of other factors may also influence parenting and child discipline. Cultural differences may dictate what type of parenting strategy is going to be successful. In some cultures, for example, public praise is not rewarding; rather it is embarrassing and may be viewed as punishment. If a stepparent should marry into such a culture, understanding these types of differences will be absolutely essential.

Poverty has negative effects on families and leads to much family stress. In fact, poverty is positively correlated with corporal punishment as well as child abuse. Religious values and health issues can also influence parental behavior. Be sure to ask each family whether there are any environmental, religious, cultural, or health issues that may influence parenting.

This exercise is primarily a general group discussion about how all of these other variables can influence parenting and child discipline. Ask the parents specifically about how religious, cultural, health, or socioeconomic variables might tend to influence parenting. Also, ask how the structure of the family—single-parent, blended, or traditional—will influence the family.

Conclusion

Each parent or set of parents is unique. The same is true of each child. Furthermore, the addition of each child changes the family. Strategies that worked with the oldest child may not work with the second or third child. Successful parents carefully consider many variables—their personalities, their children's temperament and developmental status, cultural values, religious values, and the overall environmental setting. Parents' personality styles dictate which types of disciplinary solutions will be most comfortable and compatible. Children's temperaments and developmental stages govern attentiveness, mood, comprehension, and to a certain extent, compliance. Effective parenting involves taking all of these variables into careful consideration and then selecting appropriate interventions. Encourage parents to consider at least three possible solutions for a given problem. They can then implement the one that shows the most promise. If after four weeks of consistent, unfailing follow-through there are no signs of behavioral change, they should to try another solution. One will eventually work better than the others.

Then ask them to record how many times each day the target behavior occurs. This recording will be in two phases. During the baseline phase, there are no consequences, so the consequences column is blank for those seven days. During the intervention phase, parents record the frequency of the target behaviors and how many times the planned intervention occurred. This helps them monitor their own behavior.

Target behaviors can be defined either positively or negatively. For example, "Obeying the first time asked" is a positive description; "Not obeying the first time asked" is a negative description. Whenever possible, encourage the use of the positive perspective.

The chart for Bob and Tammy's children (Handout 8, page 68) shows daily compliance ranged from 2 to 9 during the baseline. During the first three weeks of interventions, cooperation ranged from 4 to 33—a nice improvement. Notice also that Bob and Tammy were very consistent in making sure that consequences were consistent.

Materials Needed

- Handout 9: Parenting Styles
- Handout 10: Temperament
- Handout 11: Growth and Development

Habit 4

Communicating Openly

Purpose

The purpose of this session is to help peaceful parents develop a pattern of parent-child communication that reflects empathy, caring, and respect.

What Parents Will Learn

1. Assertive, nonblaming approaches for giving corrective feedback to children, effective ways of giving genuine and positive feedback, and how to give "I" messages when communicating

2. To communicate empathically with their children

3. The importance of and how to conduct regular family meetings

4. More creative ways of communicating with their children

Background for the Facilitator: Caring Communication

Peaceful parents recognize the need for responding to the entire spectrum of child communication—actions, words, and feelings. Effective parents let their children know they understand their feelings. They are sensitive to the feelings that are often implicit in their children's communications. Parents can further build their relationships with their children by learning to share both positive and negative feelings in constructive ways. They also set reasonable expectations for themselves and their children in terms of sharing and communicating. In addition, they recognize the importance of regular family meetings. In family meetings, negotiation and conflict-resolution skills are paramount. Furthermore, peaceful parents use creative ways of communicating with their children including Post-its, covert messages, and metaphors. Parents are skilled at giving corrective feedback without communicating ego-crushing disappointment.

In the initial part of this session, ask parents to share with the group the family communication styles prevalent in their family. Ask them to discuss whether they have used family meetings and how they have been organized. Finally, ask them to talk about how they have tried to use more effective means of communication with their children.

- Love and caring can be communicated in many different ways.

- Self-disclosure is important in building relationships with children.

- Corrective feedback can be given without crushing egos.

- Empathic communication helps build child-parent relationships.

Session Plan

In this session, six different communication skills will be discussed: communicating love and caring, active listening, self-disclosing, communicating creatively, using statements rather than questions, and running family meetings. Some group exercises will be used to introduce four of the skills. The information on creative communicating and turning questions into statements will be presented in a brief lecture format.

■ Exercise 1:
Communicating Love and Caring

Enhancing parental communication skills is important for developing and nurturing a child's self-esteem. Parents can develop a number of skills for this purpose. First, they can learn how to communicate love and unconditional positive support. There are many ways of showing love and acceptance toward children. Some are verbal; others are nonverbal. The most obvious way is simply to tell children that you love them. So often parents take for granted that their children know they are loved that they actually forget to tell them. But it's important for parents to reiterate this message.

Love can also be communicated nonverbally by gestures, facial expressions, or other forms of touch. Touching, mussing a child's hair, and hugging are all nonverbal ways of building closeness and rapport. As children reach adolescence, the nature of the touching may change, but it will always be an important ingredient.

Another way of communicating love, acceptance, and regard is to show that you value what a child is saying by giving them a green light to continue. Simply nodding or saying "uh-huh" or "tell me more" communicates love, interest, and attention.

For this exercise, ask parents to pull out Handout 7, Tips for Terrific Talk (page 66). Place them in groups of two and encourage them to go through this list and identify some of the words of encouragement that could also be words of love and caring. In the dyadic setting, they will practice about a half-dozen of these statements.

■ Exercise 2:
Active Listening

In addition to communicating love and regard for their children, parents also benefit from listening accurately and attentively, especially for implied feelings. For many years, psychologists have demonstrated that children who feel understood and who are comfortable in expressing their feelings and thoughts in a relationship come to value and prize that relationship. This also leads to trust and feelings of safety. Helping a child realize he has been heard and understood is very important in terms of building the relationship with a parent and of developing self-esteem. When children feel understood, they feel important, worthwhile, and valued.

That is why we teach parents the fundamentals of active listening. Active or reflective listening helps the parents understand how the child is feeling and then let the child know he or she is understood by communicating those feelings back to the child. Sometimes the word *mirroring* is used. To understand what children are feeling, parents have to listen to more than the actual words. They need to listen to the tone of voice and to recognize the context within which the child is making the comment. It has been suggested that understanding a child's feelings is like listening to a song—the parents have to pay attention to the music as well as the words. Simply recognizing the feelings, however, is not sufficient, and does not really nurture the relationship. Sharing with the child the realization that the parent understands the feelings is what brings closeness.

During the presentation, use many examples and model reflective responses. Reflective responses involve a number of sentence stems including, "You sure sound _____," "You feel _____," "You would really like to _____" (Handout 12, page 73, top half). For activities, divide the parents into groups of three. Have ready a variety of prepared situations written on cards. Ask the parent who is playing the role of a child to read the card and the parent who is playing the role of the parent to respond empathically. The observer or coach assists the "parent" in providing feedback about how empathic and how accurate the responses seem. The "child" should also give feedback to the parent. It's helpful to use an empathic vocabulary sheet so parents have a good idea of the range of empathic responses (Handout 13, page 74).

■ Exercise 3: Self-Disclosure

A third basic communication skill is self-disclosure or "I" message communication (Handout 12, page 73, bottom half). With this type of communication, parents express their own feelings in a way that is less threatening, less judgmental, and void of name calling. It focuses on the child's behavior and the parental reaction to it. It involves honest communication on the part of the parent and the child. As an example: "Nathan, when your bike is in the driveway, I can't drive into the garage. As a result, I feel annoyed. Please remember to keep the driveway clear."

Although "I" message communication is often discussed in a context of giving corrective feedback it can also be used to give positive specific feedback, which is helpful in nurturing good self-concept. "Breanna, studying hard for your math test really paid off. I'm so proud of you!" "I" message communication is constructive, not destructive, communication. It focuses on anger control and minimizes blame. "I" message communication involves using the word *I* as the subject of the sentence. Most destructive and blaming types of communication begin the sentence with the word *You.* In "I" message communication, the parent first shares the feeling and then expresses which behavior of the child leads to the feeling. Often the parent requests a change in behavior. For example, the parent could say, "Billy, I feel annoyed when

I'm interrupted as I am trying to fix dinner. Please ask me those questions later." Again, lead the parents in role-playing, using groups of three. Present a variety of prepared situations, and the parents can practice sharing behavior (Handout 14, page 75).

■ Exercise 4:
The Magic of Language

Demonstrate how metaphors and covert language can enhance communication. Many children are well versed in the language of athletics, and parents can often use sports-related words to facilitate meaning and to establish rapport. For example, to help a child hold his or her temper better, the parent can use a baseball metaphor: "When a ball is hit, you catch it and then you hold it."

■ Exercise 5:
Statements, Not Questions

Help parents change questions into statements. Oftentimes, parents ask questions to which they already know the answers to entrap the child. The result is often anger and destructive communication. Instead of saying, "What time did you get in last night?" (when the parent knows exactly what time the child got in), he or she might say, "I know you got home at 1:45 A.M. This is an hour and forty-five minutes later than our agreed-on time. We need to talk about that."

■ Exercise 6:
The Family Meeting

In role-playing, the family meeting demonstrates a number of features. First of all, ground rules need to be established (Handout 15, page 76). Each meeting should deal with one topic. A suggested ground rule is that the speaker is to be respected with no interrupting. Every family member needs to be in control. One way to assure this is through the use of a talking stick. Each participant takes a turn with the stick while everyone else listens attentively. Everyone should use "I" language, not "You" language. Remind parents that in the "I" language format, the speaker takes responsibility for his or her feelings, whereas in the "You" language format, the other person is blamed. All solutions suggested in the family meetings should be respected and considered. If no agreement can be reached for an urgent issue, the parents may decide the answer. If the issue is less urgent, the topic can be brought up at the next family meeting. At the end of the meeting, a time and a place for the next family meeting should be specified.

In demonstrating the family meeting, play the parent while the parent participants act as the children. Make sure that throughout all of the exercises, nonverbal language is congruent with the overt verbal message. You may need to use numerous examples of how children's interests and hobbies may be a basis for metaphorical language. Model and encourage the generous use of humor. In the role-plays, encourage the parents to praise each other. Then compliment and praise parents for their efforts and improvements. In addition, show parents how to use animated nonverbals for positive feedback and few, if any, nonverbals for corrective feedback. Throughout, stress that corrective feedback is brief and to the point, while positive feedback tends to be more wordy.

Note: Ask parents to briefly review their Behavior Charts to track changes in the behavior they identified at the beginning of the program.

Conclusion

Effective communication nurtures the parent-child relationship. Examples include conveying love and caring, listening empathically, and self-disclosing. With internal motivation and external guidance and feedback, parents can learn to change their communication habits.

At the end of the session, hand out the Important vs. Urgent Quadrant Sheet (Handout 16, page 77), so that the parents may review it before the next session.

Materials Needed

- Cards demonstrating sample situations to be used for the communication exercises

- A sheet that each family can use for generating the rules for the family meeting

- Handout 7: Tips for Terrific Talk

- Handout 12: Active Listening Stems and "I" Message Statements

- Handout 13: Feeling Words

- Handout 14: Communication Exercises

- Handout 15: Ground Rules for Family Meetings

- Handout 16: "Important vs. Urgent" Quadrant Sheet

Habit 5

Nurturing Your Child's Self-Esteem

Purpose

The purpose of this session is to help parents enhance their child's self-concept by setting priorities and attending to specific behaviors that influence a child's self-image.

What Parents Will Learn

1. To categorize activities, issues, and values along the urgent/not urgent and important/not important dimensions as they pertain to self-concept

2. The importance of a good self-concept

3. How specific behaviors directly influence a child's self-esteem

Background for the Facilitator: Developing a Good Self-Concept

Self-concept can be considered a collection of the thoughts and feelings people have about themselves—who they are, what their values are, what their abilities are, and anything that makes them special. People with good self-concept feel competent, important, and worthwhile. Those who have a poor self-concept feel unimportant, inadequate, and incompetent. A child's success and happiness depend on self-concept. Parents are the most significant individuals in forming a child's self-concept and they need to understand how their actions and words can do that.

All of us, children included, need to feel that we are valued, worthwhile, and lovable. This aspect of self-concept has a great influence on future interactions and relationships. Those who feel lovable and valued tend to love and value others as well. Parents, peers, and other important people in a child's life communicate either love and value, or criticism and rejection. A child's feelings and thoughts about himself or herself are acquired through interactions with significant other people. The way parents and other significant people communicate with children influences how children feel about themselves. Parents and significant others contribute love and value both verbally and nonverbally. They can do it with words, body language, and facial expressions. Also, being able to understand a child's feelings is an important aspect of communicating love, acceptance, and value. Discipline and corrective feedback can be communicated without devaluing or denigrating the value of the child. One goal of peaceful parenting is to communicate love and value, and to give corrective feedback in such a way that self-esteem is preserved.

In addition to feeling valued, loved, and worthwhile, children need to believe they are competent and responsible. Children acquire feelings of competence and responsibility through certain kinds of successful experiences in which they learn to solve a variety of problems. Competent children feel they have the skills, knowledge, and experience to cope with a variety of challenges, whether they are interpersonal or otherwise. They believe they can influence their surrounding world or environment in an effective manner. As children acquire these problem-solving skills, they should receive positive feedback both from themselves and from significant others. This gives them the confidence to try new experiences and to learn new skills. Many parents walk the fine line between doing too much for their children and doing too little. Parents need to know which challenges and problems are beyond the child's skill level and which ones the child can successfully cope with. Some failure and frustration is part of the trial-and-error learning process that helps children acquire responsibility and competence. Children should realize they may fail at a new task without experiencing punishment or rejection. Experiencing failure while acquiring a new skill should not be punished. When a child fails to solve a problem they have repeatedly been able to deal with successfully in the past, corrective feedback may be needed to get them back on track. The wise parent must know the difference between these two situations. Most of the time, natural or logical consequences are feedback enough in acquiring new skills.

- Effective parental communication influences children's sense of value, worth, and caring.

- Effective parental communication helps children feel competent and responsible.

- Corrective feedback can facilitate the growth of self-esteem.

- Most important things in life are not urgent, and most urgent things in life are not important.

Session Plan

Using the quadrant sheet handed out in the last session, discuss with the participants how some families are dominated by the urgent things in life while other families tend to make decisions based on the important things in life.

Next, have parents practice beneficial ways of giving both positive and corrective feedback. Parents will also learn how certain social skills can enhance self-esteem.

■ Exercise 1:
Completing the Quadrant Sheet

Give parents a blank quadrant sheet (Handout 16, page 77). Have them examine their interactions with their children during the past week, and ask them to place the interactions in the appropriate quadrants (urgent/not urgent versus important/not important). With the parents, analyze the grids to determine where the family spends the greater amount of their time and energy. Have parents work in small groups to formulate how they can free up more energy for the important but not urgent things in life, especially self-concept. Help them realize that directing energy into the important things in life, especially enhancing self-concept, is part of the process of becoming a peacemaker in the family.

■ Exercise 2:
Helpful Encouragement

Parents need to realize that appropriate positive feedback can nurture self-esteem and self-concept (Handout 7, page 66). Praise and encouragement are most helpful when they describe specific behaviors or actions that were appropriate and pleasing. Global positive statements, such as "You are such a good girl," tend to be less helpful and in some cases can actually induce guilt. Helpful, appropriate positive feedback specifies what the child did and also the positive effect it had on other people. Ask parents to list different kinds of praise and encouragement and help them determine how they are beneficial. (See Handout 17, Positive Feedback, page 78.)

■ Exercise 3:
Corrective Feedback That Helps Children Feel Worthwhile and Valued

Help parents realize that corrective feedback is necessary and helpful, but that it can also be harmful. It's usually best when it's specific and focuses on the undesirable behavior and its effects on others, while safeguarding the child's self-worth and value. It's beneficial when it contains suggestions for an alternative decision or course of behavior that would have resulted in a more favorable outcome. Encouragement and helpful corrective feedback build self-esteem, whereas unhelpful praise and critical corrective feedback result in lowered self-esteem. Parents should monitor their own behavior by asking, "Will what I am doing or saying now help my child to believe that they are more worthwhile, more valued, and more loved?"

An example of helpful corrective feedback is as follows: "Chris, I asked you not to color with the markers after you took your bath and put on clean clothes. Now, your hands and clothes are all colored with markers and you will need to wash and change your clothes. I like to be on time for church. Now we will have to rush and I do not like to do that. Next time, please do what I ask you to."

Using the Corrective Feedback 1 handout (Handout 17, page 78), ask parents to write out some hypothetical corrective statements from real-life experiences that would allow their child to feel loved and valued.

■ Exercise 4:
Corrective Feedback That Helps Children Feel Responsible and Competent

Another activity is to help parents learn to give beneficial corrective feedback to their children in a way that still allows them to feel responsible and competent. Parents can help their children gain self-confidence and problem-solving skills by pointing out the consequences of their behaviors. (See Handout 17, page 78.) Consequences should be mentioned in a matter-of-fact, educational manner, not in a punitive or harsh way. For example, "Pete, I guess you didn't put the lid back on your marker and now it is all dried up so you won't be able to draw anymore with it." Or, "Katie, your toys were left out and the dogs thought they were their toys and chewed them all up, so you won't be able to play the game you wanted to." In general, parents can monitor their own behavior by asking themselves, "Is the way I am giving feedback to my children helping them to feel more competent and responsible?"

Using Handout 17, Corrective Feedback 2, have parents write down some corrective statements based on real-life experiences that will allow their children to continue to feel responsible and competent, even though they have been given corrective feedback.

■ Exercise 5: Building Social Skills

Parents can also help their children acquire a feeling of competence and success by carefully arranging for experiences that result in competency and success. For example, children may be taught basic social skills such as introducing themselves, asking information about others, and giving compliments to facilitate making new friends. Arranging for children to participate in sports and other extracurricular activities at an appropriate level can also facilitate the feelings of competence and success. (See list Social Skills, Handout 18, page 79.)

Note: Ask parents to briefly review their Behavior Charts to track changes in the behavior they identified at the beginning of the program.

Conclusion

Early in children's lives, self-esteem is primarily influenced by feedback from their parents. In this session, parents learned that there are beneficial ways to give both positive and corrective feedback to children. Children's self-esteem is also influenced by experiences of competency. One important area of competency involves social skills. By paying attention to these factors, parents can assist children in developing a healthy self-view.

Materials Needed

- Handout 7: Tips for Terrific Talk
- Handout 16: Important vs. Urgent Quadrant Sheet
- Handout 17: Positive Feedback, Corrective Feedback 1, and Corrective Feedback 2
- Handout 18: Social Skills

Habit 6

Spending Quality Time With Your Children

Purpose

The purpose of the session is to help parents understand the importance of spending quality time building a relationship with their children.

What Parents Will Learn

1. Some of the unique ingredients and benefits of spending quality time with their children

2. How to initiate and how to end good quality time

3. How to interact with their children without using questions and directives

Background for the Facilitator: Positive Attending and Quality Time

The stronger the quality of the parent-child relationship, the smaller the amount of coercion that a parent must use to obtain compliance and cooperation. We often use the analogy of a relationship savings account. When parents are able to share appreciation, attention, respect, and love with their children, it's like putting money into a bank account. When conflicts arise, some of the savings must be withdrawn to deal with the situation. When there are few good feelings left in the account, parents must resort to more coercion and force to obtain compliance.

The rationale is to make as many deposits in the bank as possible, so in the long run withdrawals will be simpler. It's interesting to note that the larger the account, the smaller the withdrawals are. The smaller the account, the larger the withdrawals have to be in order to obtain compliance and cooperation. (See The Relationship Savings Account, Handout 19, page 80.)

One measure of the amount of goodwill in the bank is the quality of the affectionate messages the child sends to the parent. Children develop their own ways of letting their parents know that they love them. When these signs are not forthcoming, we have an indication that the bank account is not full. Keep in mind that children show affection in play, seeking parental assistance, sharing their accomplishments with them, imitating the parent's behavior, and showing them things that they have done.

A sign that the bank account is not full often occurs when parental expectations are unreasonable. An example would be a parent expecting a two-year-old to be able to understand logical reasoning.

Another indication reserves in the bank account are getting low is when molehills become mountains. In other words, small incidents become huge catastrophic events. For example, if a glass of spilled milk erupts into an hour-long tirade, things are getting out of hand.

An additional sign of a deficient savings account is the quality of the messages the parents send to the children. If the messages are damaging to the child's self-esteem or self-concept, that's a good sign there is not a lot of savings in the bank. This is often indicated by name calling, sarcasm, shaming, and blaming.

Finally, if the parents have to use a great deal of force, whether verbal or physical, this probably indicates bankruptcy. Remember, when the bank account balance is high, most discipline can be handled by very low withdrawals and when the account is near bankruptcy, disciplinary action results in very large amounts of savings withdrawals.

- Positive attending increases the balance in the relationship savings account.

- Large balances usually require mild corrective interventions.

- Low balances usually require large corrective measures.

Session Plan

This session focuses on building the parent-child relationship by spending quality time with children on a regular basis and by making sure that positive interactions outnumber negative ones.

■ Exercise 1: Positive Attending

In today's hectic world, it is difficult for parents to prioritize their daily schedule to allow for quality family time on a daily basis. One of the most effective ways of improving quality time is to work on enhancing parent-attending skills. This process focuses on parents paying attention to their children's desirable behavior and at some point becoming a participant in it. In the beginning, the parent simply finds a time when the child is playing with something that is enjoyable and appropriate. It's important for the child to select the type of play and for the parent not to influence that decision. In the session, the parent is to be relaxed and simply watch the activities for a few minutes and then sit down next to the child. For a younger child, this might involve playing house. For an older child, it could mean playing a video game. Before saying anything, the parent monitors the child's behavior to get some idea of what is really going on. Next, the parent describes what the child is doing in a simple fashion. One strategy is for the parent to pretend that he or she is a radio sportscaster at some athletic event or that there is a blind person in the room and to simply describe what the child is doing. The parent narrates what is going on and does not offer any evaluation or judgment. During this quality play time, the parent asks no questions and gives no directions.

This is one of the most important and difficult parts for parents. Of course, if the child's behavior becomes totally inappropriate, the parent may need to intervene and provide some directives. The parent could also offer some genuine positive feedback. For example, he or she might say, "I really like it when we play together quietly like this."

If misbehavior occurs, the parent should look away and totally ignore it. If it escalates or continues, then the play should stop. If necessary, there may need to be some sort of a consequence, but in most cases the parent simply leaves. Ideally, each parent spends ten to twenty minutes with each child each day.

The primary purpose of positive attending is to improve the relationship between parents and children. In the process, children realize their parents are interested in them and they also give them positive feedback about their activities. Parents are not in their typical home role during this time; there are no skills or facts they have to teach. The purpose is simply to be together as two human beings, with the parent offering the child attention and positive feedback—not focused necessarily on what the child is doing, but rather on the parent's enjoyment in being with the child. In the process, the parent should resist the temptation to ask questions or to give directions, both of which place the child on the defensive. Many parents are tempted to ask questions because they find children are cooperative and attentive during this time, and the parent may want to find out about school or other things. Be sure to avoid this.

Sometimes parents feel positive attention isn't important because it is not really focusing on solving a problem. In fact, it can be more important than actually coming up with a solution to a problem. Positive attending focuses on establishing a relationship of trust and confidence, and in that atmosphere, compliance and cooperation is much more likely to happen.

Once parents have learned to attend positively to simple play, it becomes easier for them to pay attention to the child's compliance throughout the day. For example, the parent may say, "I really like it when you cooperate" or "Thanks for doing what I asked you to do." (See Handout 20, Model Statements, page 81.)

Establish triads to role-play. One parent is the child, another the attending parent, and the third the coach. Encourage the people role-playing the parents to comment on the special time together by saying, for example, "I really liked our special time together. Let's do it again."

Be alert for parental questions or directives. Sometimes it helps to videotape these interactions so parents can see themselves trying to attend positively without the use of directives or questions. Many times, parents are simply unaware of their subconscious tendency to use questions and directives.

Remind parents they should try to find at least ten to twenty minutes daily for each child. This always works best on a one-to-one basis. The activities should be noncompetitive for the most part, although in some cases, mild competition may work. Ideally, parents should keep a log of their quality time activities with their children for at least two weeks.

■ Exercise 2:
Building a Bank Account

Use the handout with ten scenarios (Handout 21, page 82) that capture child-parent communication. Read each situation and determine whether the interaction is an indication of a "deposit" or a "withdrawal" to the bank account.

Note: Ask parents to briefly review their Behavior Charts to track changes in the problem identified at the beginning of the program.

Conclusion

Spending quality time with each child is essential for developing a healthy parent-child relationship. If at all possible, each parent should spend at least twenty meaningful minutes daily with each child, one on one. In single-parent families or in families with many children, this is challenging. During this brief time, parents should refrain from asking questions or giving directions. Making sure that relationship deposits outnumber withdrawals is also very important.

Materials Needed

- Handout 3: Blank Congnitive Diary Sheets
- Handout 19: The Relationship Savings Account
- Handout 20: Model Statements
- Handout 21: Ten Parent-Child Situations

Habit 7

Disciplining in a Consistent Manner

Purpose

The purpose of this session is to help parents become more consistent in disciplining their children.

What Parents Will Learn

1. To be consistent individually, but also as a parental team

2. That their children learn through the consequences of their actions

3. To set appropriate expectations for children, which need to be clear, specific, and concise

Background for the Facilitator: Consistency Counts

Peaceful parenting strategies, which rely on consistency, predictability, and reliability, may not work as quickly as corporal punishment. Nonviolent discipline, however, is not contaminated by fear, hate, and low self-esteem. Instead, children learn desirable behaviors and are discouraged from engaging in undesirable behaviors by nonviolent means. Parents and other adults teach and influence children immeasurably. This teaching often occurs through imitation of adult behavior. Children are more likely to imitate adults when the example is consistent and when children can see benefits from engaging in the behavior.

Another way of teaching children how to behave is linked to the kind of consequences we bring about. If, for example, we run to a child's room during the night every time she cries, we are teaching that child that "If I cry, they will come." Because parents and children have an especially close relationship, parents are very powerful teachers of their own children. Parents can teach a child to decrease undesirable behavior by actively ignoring the behavior. They can also decrease a behavior by making sure that undesirable consequences occur whenever the child engages in the behavior. They can increase a behavior by making sure positive consequences occur.

Consistency is a primary component of influencing a child's behavior. For many children, if tantrums in a store result in a candy bar only once in every ten trips, that is sufficient to teach the child that "If I tantrum, I will get a candy bar." The one candy bar is more powerful than the nine times the child went away empty-handed. Consistency, accordingly, requires that the parent engage in the same behavior time after time after time. When children can predict what is going to happen, we can be reasonably assured that the teaching has occurred.

- Peaceful parenting minimizes fear, hate, and low self-esteem.
- Children imitate adults.
- Consistent consequences ensure learning.
- Rewards earned are rewards kept.

Session Plan

Engage the participants by asking them to brainstorm and identify factors that might help improve consistency, predictability, and reliability. It will be important to write these on the board or flip chart. Here are four helping strategies to try.

1. *Write it down.* Many parents have difficulty being consistent by themselves. They have even more difficulty being consistent as a parenting team. For optimal learning and discipline, however, parental consistency is extremely important. Many parents tend to act unilaterally without consulting the other partner. Feeling left out of the decision making, the other parent may directly or indirectly sabotage or contradict the disciplinary efforts of the first parent. As a result, we strongly suggest parents formulate disciplinary plans in writing with agreed-on consequences. This helps ensure that consistency, reliability, and predictability are more likely to happen. So often, parents overreact to a disciplinary situation and come up with a consequence that is far in excess of what is warranted. Predetermined written consequences, however, tend to decrease the likelihood of overreaction. Mild consequences that occur consistently, predictably, and reliably are much more powerful than intense, inconsistent, randomly occurring consequences.

2. *Break it down.* Consistency, predictability, and reliability are frequently threatened because parents won't break behavioral change into small necessary steps. Effective discipline often requires micromanagement. A comprehensive behavioral program will identify the long-term goal and will also specify short-term intermediate goals. Effective parents break down desired behaviors into small steps with specified consequences at each level. These are necessary, but not sufficient, steps in terms of peaceful parenting. Parents also need to focus on communication skills such as "I" messages, sharing, and active listening. Consistency, predictability, and reliability are more feasible and realistic when behaviors are discussed in a specific and concrete fashion. The more vague a behavior is, the more difficult it is to be consistent. The more specific and concrete a behavioral description is, the greater the likelihood of consistent follow-through.

3. *Use positive attending.* Again, we emphasize using encouragement and rewards rather than consequences. Rewards have few undesirable side effects, whereas consequences can have many. In general, ignoring or simply withholding rewards is the least damaging corrective consequence. However, ignoring has to be consistent,

which is a difficult challenge for parents. An intermittent reinforcement schedule keeps gamblers coming back to the roulette wheels and slot machines. Even a few lapses in ignoring behavior may have a similar impact on the child. Therefore, parents need to be realistic about the type of ignoring they can use.

4. *Keep accurate records*. This is one way to help improve consistency, predictability, and reliability. When parents have to chart their own behaviors and consequences, they seem better able to follow through with a consistent program. The more attentive people are to their own behaviors, the more attentive they are to the consequences of their behaviors. Until we are aware of the consequences of our behaviors, we are less likely to engage in conscious change.

To summarize the sequences of using behavioral principles, we recommend that positive consequences be used with rigorous consistency and reliability. If this fails, then use ignoring or the withdrawal of reinforcers. As a last resort, we recommend the use of actual punishment. To help improve consistency, parents should practice counting behavioral frequencies, perhaps their own behaviors as well as those of the children. Older children can use simple charts to keep track of behaviors.

■ Exercise: Establishing Expectations

Before parents establish formal behavioral change programs for their children, they must identify mutual expectations for them. Once the expectations are agreed on, the next logical step is to formulate the development of a family learning environment, which will help achieve these expectations.

Each parent may have different expectations. Therefore, they need to compromise and negotiate to establish a mutually agreed-on set of expectations and consequences. Remember, there are relatively few rights and wrongs in parenting—what is important is that the parents agree.

Determine how congruent and harmonious parenting teams are by asking them to write down, without talking to each other, their expectations and procedures for dealing with hypothetical situations. Present the ten scenarios in Handout 22, Expectations, page 83. Ask each parent to write down what he or she would expect, taking each child's developmental level into account. Then ask them to formulate a very specific and concrete behavioral plan to reach this expectation, making sure to break down the goals into small steps.

Note: Ask parents to briefly review their Behavior Charts to track changes in the behavior they identified at the beginning of the program.

Conclusion

Throughout the lesson, remind parents that the most important ways we learn are through imitation and consequences. Use brainstorming techniques to help identify roadblocks to consistency, predictability, and reliability. Like all human beings, children learn through consistent consequences of their actions. Appropriate expectations for children need to be clear, specific, and concise. Although parents have different personalities, they need to be interchangeable in the discipline of their children. This means it won't make any difference whether Mom is there or Dad is there. When desirable or undesirable actions occur, the children can expect the same feedback from either parent. Children often split parents or put a wedge between them, which results in compromised consistency.

We're more likely to continue to do activities that result in favorable and enjoyable consequences; and we're more likely to discontinue an activity that results in unfavorable consequences. To be consistent and reliable, parents should remember that rewards earned are rewards kept. When parents are implementing unfavorable consequences, they should try to take something away that the child has not earned through a reward system.

Materials Needed

- Chalkboard or newsprint pad for brainstorming on roadblocks to consistency, predictability, and reliability

- Handout 22: Expectations

Wrapping It Up

*I*n the peaceful parenting program, each session focuses on specific skills that are designed to improve the quality of the parent-child interaction and parental discipline. At the end of the sessions, you need to evaluate how well the program works. This analysis will determine whether:

1. The seven cardinal habits have been acquired.

2. Parents have acquired the skills to better handle their angry feelings.

3. Successful brainstorming and problem solving has occurred.

4. Expectations and solutions reflect the individual developmental levels and personalities of the children.

5. Parents are using respectful and effective communication strategies.

6. Parents are focusing on the important issues in parenting and are not getting sidetracked by the urgencies of daily living.

7. The parent-child relationship promises to be nourished daily through quality time and positive attending.

8. Parental strategies are pursued in a consistent, predictable, and reliable fashion.

9. Individual outcome programs help parents realize that progress is occurring in small but consistent increments.

The role of evaluation in the peaceful parenting program has two primary components. First, facilitators evaluate the skills the parents have acquired. Second, parents evaluate the effectiveness of their own specific behavioral interventions for their children.

Facilitators should complete assessments on more than one occasion. It is often beneficial to obtain a premeasure. This is the baseline data against which subsequent information can be compared. Next, measure the knowledge that the parents have acquired right after the program has been finished. Then have a follow-up measure three to six months later. This follow-up gives a better view of the true impact the program has had on the parenting behavior.

Outcome evaluations assessing knowledge can often be straightforward. Develop your own questionnaire, using true-and-false, multiple-choice, or fill-in-the-blank questions. Some evaluators might find that true-and-false questionnaires are simpler. Others might like multiple-choice formats. See Handout 23 (page 84) for an example.

Although it's difficult and time-consuming to observe parental behavior, it is essential. Since it's not going to be possible to observe actual parent-child interactions, the behavioral observations should be based upon role-playing. Establish structured scenarios that call for specific skills and use a formal rating scale. The behavioral observations should be concrete, focusing on nonverbal behaviors like eye contact, touching, smiles, gestures, and so on.

A number of developed observational programs can be used. In our experience, these are somewhat detailed and cumbersome. A less structured format may be equally effective in assessing parental behavior.

Use self-report measures to obtain parental feedback about changes they feel they have made. This can be considered a consumer satisfaction measure in which they indicate how beneficial the program has been for them. (See Handout 24, Parent Satisfaction Measure, page 85.) Commercially available instruments for doing parent rating are more suited to formal outcome studies and may not be cost-effective for a small group.

Also assess the effectiveness of your teaching efforts. This self-feedback can help you fine-tune future classes. (See Handout 25, Facilitator Self-Assessment, page 86.)

The second main component of evaluation involves parents accurately recording children's behavior. Unless parents record behavior, they truly do not know how effective various interventions are. Without evaluation and recording, effectiveness is left up to parental whim or impression. Most of the time, simple frequency charts serve a useful purpose. The behavior is defined in a concrete fashion so that there would be a consensus among any informed adults as to exactly what behavior was being assessed. Before beginning an intervention, obtain baseline data. Then, the intervention can begin, and a simple visual review of the chart will determine whether the interventions are working.

Behavior recording is a way of assessing the benefit of multiple interventions. For example, let's suppose that Mary and Peter have a five-year-old son who has violent and destructive temper tantrums. The first step is to actually pinpoint what a tantrum is. It could be given an operational definition such as "a period of upset in which either the voice is raised for over a minute or something is thrown in frustration." Then the parents record this baseline data for approximately a week. They might decide that the first intervention will be a time-out, which occurs as soon as a tantrum begins. Then they chart that for perhaps a week or two. If they feel the tantrums have not subsided sufficiently, they might then add a positive consequence. They might say that every day there is no tantrum will result in a specific reward. For example, a child might obtain points toward a movie or a special outing. They clearly mark this in the chart, so that they can determine whether adding the reward decreases the tantrums. (See the Behavioral Plan, Handout 26, page 87.)

It often takes up to four weeks for new behaviors to settle into the desired range. Charting helps parents realize that behavioral changes do not occur instantaneously and helps them see and appreciate little bits of progress. It's also a way for parents to stay on task. If parents have enough motivation to maintain a behavior chart, they most likely have enough motivation to be consistent and reliable in implementing consequences. Reviewing the behavioral charts gives a good measure of parental motivation. (See the Behavior Recording Chart, Handout 8, pages 67–68.)

If the parents determine that sufficient progress has not occurred with the selected consequences, then they can change the consequences and continue charting.

Evaluation Activities

Develop a test or a questionnaire to ensure that some basic acquisition of knowledge has occurred regarding the seven habits of peaceful parenting. Use behavioral observations to make sure that the parents are able to put the knowledge gained into action. And use the behavior charts to remind parents that Rome was not built in a day. This also serves as a basis for helping parents understand that parenting is a trial-and-error process. Sometimes, when a change is made, behavior gets worse before it gets better. The use of the behavior chart helps parents see this. All in all, if change has not occurred within four weeks, then the solution or consequences should be changed. Just as you use evaluation to determine whether the program is working, parents should do regular review to make sure their family is moving in the desired direction.

The Peaceful Parenting Support Group

After the formal Peaceful Parenting Training Program is completed, parents may want to form an ongoing support group. A support group provides a forum for networking, actual support, and possibly continuing education opportunities. In the forum, parents might present and discuss clips from various video programs or handouts they have run across. They also might have an informal in-service program. Knowledgeable persons in the community might be asked to present a topic of interest to all. This can keep the support group exciting and viable.

Ideally, a couple, or in some cases perhaps just a single parent or two, should be the parent leaders. If at all possible, there should also be a professional adviser with whom the parent facilitators may consult. This may actually be the facilitator who guided the parents in the first place, or someone else. If possible, the support group should meet at the same time every month. While it may be possible to meet in a facility that donates space to support groups, such as a church or hospital, it may also be possible to meet in the homes of members. The parent facilitators may meet with the professional adviser to plan an agenda for the meeting. The agenda should consider the needs, interests, and expectations of all parent participants. It would be nice to involve each of the parent members in some voluntary capacity. Above all, it is important to plan to have refreshments. The parent facilitator needs to have the skills to establish a very comfortable, relaxed environment. The parent members should feel confident in speaking and should have trust in their leader.

The support group should help parents become even more successful and gain even more confidence. Parents should be praised for sharing information and for their continued hard work along the journey of parenting. People need to feel important, included, and valuable in the group. A good sense of humor will help everyone get past the rough times. It's important for the parent facilitator to have the names, addresses, and phone numbers of all the members so members can be kept informed.

Materials Needed

- Handout 8: Behavior Recording Chart
- Handout 23: Parent Pre/Post Test
- Handout 24: Parent Satisfaction Measure
- Handout 25: Facilitator Self-Assessment
- Handout 26: Behavioral Plan

Appendix

Handouts

Peaceful Parenting

Classes begin

_____

and are held at

_____.

The sessions are 2 hours long.

Baby-sitting available.

Transportation if needed.

Call _____

with questions.

 From *The Seven Habits of Peaceful Parents* by Dr. Joseph Cress, Dr. Elizabeth Lonning, and Burt Berlowe.

Unrealistic
Self-Statements

1. Children should be seen and not heard.

2. Every time children are finished playing with their toys, they should put them away.

3. If children aren't responsible, they will grow up to be irresponsible adults.

4. Messy children grow up to be messy adults.

5. Children always need to obey their parents.

6. Parents are always right.

7. Children cannot show anger or sadness because this means they disrespect their parents.

8. When children are told to do something, they must do it immediately.

9. Children should always get along with each other.

10. A parent should know how to deal with their children in each and every situation.

11. If a child is bad, it means that the parents have failed.

12. A rule is a rule and there are no exceptions.

Realistic
Self-Statements

1. I would like her to be neater, but this is something that will improve with time.

2. I would like him to work harder in school and get good grades so he can be successful in the future. I realize, however, good grades aren't everything.

3. His behavior is upsetting to me and embarrasses me, but it doesn't seem to bother anybody else.

4. Even though he tends to be reckless, he doesn't seem to hurt anybody or destroy anything, so maybe I need to relax a bit.

5. I guess sometimes things just don't go the way we want them to or the way we planned.

6. I wish he could share his true feelings with me, but I know the more upset I get, the less likely he is able to do so.

 From *The Seven Habits of Peaceful Parents* by Dr. Joseph Cress, Dr. Elizabeth Lonning, and Burt Berlowe.

Cognitive Diary

To aid in the management of anger, it is helpful to identify the thought processes behind our behavior or anger so we can begin to change our thoughts in an effort to alter our behavior. This technique will also be beneficial in building positive perspectives of others' behavior (e.g., *"Maybe they had a long day, too"*).

Trigger Event	Distorted/Exaggerated Thoughts	Alternative Thoughts	Parent's Response/Behavior
Example: Children will not pick up their toys.	*Example:* "I've had a long day, why can't they just mind? They should mind me; I'm their parent!"	*Example:* "Maybe they can sense my stress of the long day. We *all* just need to have some quiet time and leave the toys until later."	*Example (Before Alternative Thoughts):* "You kids never do what I ask you to do—I don't ask that much." *(yelling)* *Example (After Alternative Thoughts):* "As soon as we get these toys picked up we can have supper. Let's see how fast we can get it done!"

From *The Seven Habits of Peaceful Parents* by Dr. Joseph Cress, Dr. Elizabeth Lonning, and Burt Berlowe.
Handout 3

ABCs of Anger Management

A. Apologize. Admit that you made a mistake, used poor judgment, or acted hastily in response to a "trigger."

B. Be Brief. Don't overdo your responses. Keep them to a few sentences.

C. Change What You Can. Solve the problems you can, and live with those you can't fix.

D. Deal with the Here and Now. Don't be a historian, dragging up all the transgressions from the past. Focus instead on the immediate situation.

E. Early Warning Signs of Anger/Stress. Recognize the signals of stress and act accordingly. These may include muscle tension, headaches, stomach upset, or sweating. Do whatever you can to relieve these symptoms before they get out of hand.

F. Forgive. Learn to let go of your angry feelings toward the offender, even if they don't apologize. Forgiveness is mainly for your benefit, not theirs.

G. Get Close. Stand near the other person when responding. And do it softly. Shouting or yelling only conveys anger.

H. Healthy Habits. We handle our anger better if our body is in balance and harmony. This means adequate exercise and nutrition.

I. Inner Balance. Keep a balance between the important (or urgent) demands in life and those that are less significant.

J. Just Take a Walk. Get away from the intensity of conflict and cool off.

K. Keep Your Cool. Anger is a distracter. If you are intensely angry, other people will focus on the feeling, not on what you are saying.

L. Let It Go. Don't let irritants build up. Discharge your frustrations before they accumulate.

M. Mountains vs. Molehills. How important is this event that I'm upset about? What difference will it make in a day, a week, a month from now?

N. Nurturing People. Spend time with those who are positive, uplifting, optimistic, and well nurtured.

O. Optimism not Pessimism. Focus on the bright side of things, and on what can change.

P. Prevention. Head off conflicts before they arise. When a problem comes up, work it out, so it is less likely to happen again.

Q. Quiet Place. Go to a quiet place at work, at home, or in your mind where you can regroup and re-establish a sense of peace and tranquility.

R. Reference. Know where the person you have a conflict with is coming from. With children, for example, nearly every misbehavior is an attempt to solve a problem. But we don't often ask about the problem from their point of view.

S. Step Back. By stepping back and rethinking the situation, we can respond with more insight and less anger.

T. Trial and Error. We're human beings and we make mistakes again and again. We hope that we learn from each mistake and are less likely to make it again.

U. Understanding. Anger is more complex than an emotional reaction to frustration. Most of the time, events that enrage us are other people's attempts to solve their own problems. We need to understand what those problems are and how they are affecting the other person.

V. Vent. When we are angry or fearful, it often helps to share that distress with someone else who will listen and be supportive.

W. Willing to Listen/Compromise. Few ideas are absolutely right or wrong and most have solutions. Compromise usually leads to everybody winning.

X. X-ray. Make a point to see more deeply into the attitudes and motivations of those with whom we are in conflict. Increased awareness helps to temper our responses.

Y. Yield. Be flexible enough to negotiate and accommodate. Avoid unimportant power struggles.

Z. Zone. Be sure to have that inner place of peace, harmony, and tranquility where you can go whenever you need to.

From *The Seven Habits of Peaceful Parents* by Dr. Joseph Cress, Dr. Elizabeth Lonning, and Burt Berlowe.

Summary of Behavior Strategies

1. **Brainstorming.** Generating as many solutions or ideas to a problem as possible, brainstorming may occur during a family meeting or with parents alone.

2. **Contracts.** Especially helpful with adolescents, these written agreements specify behaviors each party agrees to do. They are signed by family members with a date for reassessment.

3. **Time-Outs/Groundings.** This strategy involves time away from rewarding activities and experiences.

4. **Positive Consequences/Rewards.** These are typically pleasant or enjoyable experiences that encourage behavior.

5. **Corrective Consequences/ Punishments.** These are typically unpleasant and are to be avoided. The purpose is to decrease undesirable behavior.

6. **Encouragement and Praise.** These social reinforcers should be concrete, specific, and given as soon as possible after the desired behavior.

7. **Role of Fines.** Fines occur after an undesired behavior. Typically in small amounts, they are quite effective for impulsive kinds of behavior.

8. **Grandma's Rule.** Highly desirable behaviors are used as reinforcers for completion of less desired behaviors. For example, "As soon as you mow the lawn, you may go to your friend's house."

9. **Logical/Natural Consequences.** Natural consequences occur without outside involvement. As an example, "If you don't dress warmly, you will be cold." Logical consequences do not necessarily occur naturally, but they are reasonable. For example, if there is a fight over a toy, a logical consequence would be to put it away for a while.

10. **Conflict Resolution.** This strategy for problem-solving involves family members' brainstorming, generating many solutions to an identified problem. In a systematic fashion, solutions are eliminated one by one. At the end, one or two solutions should remain that appear to have acceptable effectiveness and approval from all family members.

11. **Family Meeting.** This is a time for sharing, discussing, deciding, evaluating, planning, and having fun. It needs to be an open forum in which all members believe they can be heard.

From *The Seven Habits of Peaceful Parents* by Dr. Joseph Cress, Dr. Elizabeth Lonning, and Burt Berlowe. Handout 5

Positive Consequences/Rewards

These are example of pleasant or enjoyable experiences that encourage desirable behavior.

- Positive statements
- Tokens or points
- Extra TV or computer time, or delayed bedtime
- Choosing dessert for a night

- Renting a video
- Extra individual parent time

Add more for your own children:

-
-
-
-

Corrective Consequences/Punishments

These are examples of typically unpleasant consequences that are designed to decrease undesirable behavior.

- Removal of privileges
- Additional chores
- Fines

- Ignoring

Add more for your own children:

-
-
-

Tips for Terrific Talk

- A-1.
- Absolutely right.
- Beautiful job.
- Clever.
- Congratulations.
- Couldn't have done it better myself.
- Dynamite.
- Excellent.
- Fantastic.
- Fine.
- Good for you.
- Good remembering.
- Good thinking.
- Great.
- I agree.
- I appreciate your help.
- I knew you could do it.
- I like that.
- I like that—I didn't know it could be done that way.
- I like the way you explained it.
- I love you.
- I'm happy to see you working like that.
- I'm proud of the way you worked today.
- I'm so proud of you.
- I'm very proud of you.
- I think you've got it now.
- Keep it up.
- Keep up the hard work.
- Let's put this somewhere special.
- Lovely.
- Marvelous.
- NATO.
- Nice going.
- Nice try.

- Nothing can stop you now.
- Now that's what I call a fine job.
- Now you have it.
- Now you have the hang of it.
- Now you're really trying.
- Now you've figured it out.
- Outstanding.
- Right on.
- Sensational.
- Super.
- Superb.
- Swell.
- Terrific.
- That shows a great deal of work.
- That shows thought.
- That *was* a good choice.
- That was very kind of you.
- That's a good point to bring up.
- That's a kind thing you did.
- That's a masterpiece.
- That's an excellent goal.
- That's clear thinking.
- That's good work.
- That's interesting.
- That's it.
- That's much better.
- That's my boy or girl.
- That's quite an improvement.
- That's really nice.
- That's right.
- That's so good.
- That's the way to do it.
- That's the way.
- That's very good.
- Tremendous.
- Way to go.

- Well done.
- Well, look at you go.
- Well thought out.
- Wonderful.
- Wonderful job.
- Wow.
- You are learning fast.
- You are really learning a lot.
- You are very good at that.
- You can do it.
- You catch on very quickly.
- You certainly did well today.
- You did a lot of work today.
- You did that very well.
- You do it very well.
- You figured that out fast.
- You haven't missed a thing.
- You make it look easy.
- You must have been practicing.
- You really make being a parent fun.
- You remembered.
- You should be very proud of this.
- You're a great help.
- You're doing beautifully.
- You're doing fine.
- You're doing the best you can.
- You're getting better every day.
- You're on the right track now.
- You're really going to town.
- You're really growing up.
- You're really improving.
- You're really working hard today.
- You've got that down pat.

 From *The Seven Habits of Peaceful Parents* by Dr. Joseph Cress, Dr. Elizabeth Lonning, and Burt Berlowe.

Behavior Recording Chart

Target Behavior _____

	(1) Day	(2) # of Times Direction Was Given	(3) # of Target Behaviors	(4) # of Times Intervention Happened
Baseline (No Consequences)	1			
	2			
	3			
	4			
	5			
	6			
	7			
Intervention (With Consequences)	8			
	9			
	10			
	11			
	12			
	13			
	14			
	15			
	16			
	17			
	18			
	19			
	20			
	21			
	22			
	23			
	24			

From *The Seven Habits of Peaceful Parents* by Dr. Joseph Cress, Dr. Elizabeth Lonning, and Burt Berlowe.

Behavior Recording Chart

Target Behavior ___*Cooperating/Listening/Obeying first time told*___

	(1) Day	(2) # of Times Direction Was Given	(3) # of Target Behaviors	(4) # of Times Intervention Happened
Baseline (No Consequences)	1	26	2	
	2	28	4	
	3	27	3	
	4	29	9	
	5	31	6	
	6	33	7	
	7	28	4	
Intervention (With Consequences)	8	30	4	26
	9	29	6	24
	10	26	8	23
	11	25	7	24
	12	35	10	33
	13	33	14	30
	14	27	18	23
	15	34	25	24
	16	30	20	26
	17	35	23	22
	18	28	19	17
	19	36	24	24
	20	24	32	21
	21	27	29	27
	22	29	30	29
	23	33	33	31
	24	30	30	30

From *The Seven Habits of Peaceful Parents* by Dr. Joseph Cress, Dr. Elizabeth Lonning, and Burt Berlowe.

Parenting Styles

- **Potters** find it easy to be consistent and often use behavioral programs. They maintain behavior charts and checklists to monitor their child's behavior.

- **Gardeners** use many preventive tactics. They believe primarily in positive feedback and rarely use corrective consequences.

- **Maestros** are very goal-oriented. They identify areas of strength and maximize them.

- **Consultants** focus on problem-solving strategies and are advisers to their children. They see themselves as partners with their children.

Handout 9   From *The Seven Habits of Peaceful Parents* by Dr. Joseph Cress, Dr. Elizabeth Lonning, and Burt Berlowe.   **69**
© 2001 Resource Publications, Inc. All rights reserved.

Temperament

Factor	Behavioral Differences		
Activity Level	• Lethargic • Sleeps quietly • Falls asleep quickly • Sits still • Walks	vs.	• Active • Tears bed covers apart • Has difficulty falling asleep • Wiggles • Runs
Rhythmicity	• Predictable patterns of eating, sleeping, and toileting	vs.	• Erratic, uneven patterns of eating, sleeping, and toileting
Adaptability *(how long to adjust)*	• Readily takes to strangers • Readily accepts new foods • Learns to follow rules easily • Likes new games • Adjusts readily after vacation	vs.	• Slow to warm up to strangers • Refuses new foods • Has a hard time comprehending rules • Resists new games • Takes a long time to get back in routines after vacation
Approach/Withdrawal *(child's initial reaction)*	• Affable • Accepts change • Confident	vs.	• Shy • Fusses, tantrums • Hesitant
Threshold Level *(sensitivity)*	• Sleeps through thunderstorms • Comments on odors and fragrances • Comments on colors, clothes • Seldom cries	vs.	• Wakes at the drop of a hat • Seems not to smell anything • Ignores • Cries and complains before anything happens (e.g., immunizations at doctor's office)
Intensity of Reaction	• Smiles quietly • Whimpers when disappointed	vs.	• Screams wildly with delight with theatrical gestures • Roars and cries when frustrated or hurt
Quality of Mood	• Contented • Usually has a miserable time • Enjoys helping others • Smiles easily and often • Optimistic • Accepting	vs.	• Discontented • Usually has a good time • Inactive, passive • Usually somber, serious • Pessimistic • Complaining
Distractibility	• Stays on task	vs.	• Easily drawn away from tasks by extraneous noises or movements
Persistence/Attention Span	• Persists with activity • Tolerates frustration when learning new tools • Returns to task after being interrupted	vs.	• Gets bored easily • Very impatient • Can't return to task after being interrupted

(Adapted from Drs. Alexander Thomas and Stella Chess, *Temperament and Development* [New York: Brenner/Mazel, 1977])

Growth and Development

Age	Characteristic Behaviors	
2	• Likes to explore • Energetic • Likes attention (positive or negative) • Can't share yet	• Fearful when parents leave • Can't reason • Likes rituals • Distractible • Inattentive
2½	• Beginning to develop language, coordination, and social learning	• Assertive and bossy • Indecisive • Preoccupied by saying "No!"
3 **(Preschool)**	• More flexible, calmer • Beginning to share • More conforming and compliant • More accepting of explanations, but still can't reason	• Ready for cooperative, interactive play • Beginning self-help activities • More tolerant
3½ **(Preschool)**	• Seems to regress • Jealous • Intrusive • Imaginary playmates • New fears • Rich fantasy and make-believe world, may seem like lying	• Beginning correlational/associative understanding (that events or activities seem to occur at about the same time), but no causal understanding (how one thing causes another)
4 **(Preschool)**	• Expansive • Energetic • Friendly • Worried	• Bathroom talk • Rich fantasy • Sassy
4½ **(Preschool)**	• Constant questioning • Better attention	• Slips in and out of the real world and the world of fantasy and make-believe
5 **(Kindergarten)**	• Calmer • More compliant • Needs routines • Like approval • Active fantasy	• More confident and secure
6 **(Kindergarten–** **1st Grade)**	• More unpredictable • Defiant • Domineering • Energetic • Insecure • Dramatic	• Competitive • Complaining • Self-preoccupied • Rapid mood changes • All-or-nothing thinking • Overreacts to parent saying "No."
7 **(1st–2nd Grades)**	• More reasonable • Less provocative • Concerned with popularity • Conscientious	• More persistent • Becomes aware of success • Expanded vocabulary

From *The Seven Habits of Peaceful Parents* by Dr. Joseph Cress, Dr. Elizabeth Lonning, and Burt Berlowe.

Growth and Development

Age	Characteristic Behaviors	
8 **(2nd–3rd Grades)**	• Uninhibited • Energetic • Overly dramatic • Wants to be self-sufficient and independent	• Seems confident/self-assured, but is still vulnerable • Develops a special or "best" friend • Sensitive to peer pressure
9 **(3rd–4th Grades)**	• More responsible • Begins to think more logically • Preoccupied with gangs and cliques • Perfectionist	• Able to concentrate • Interest in developing specific skills (music, sports, etc.) • Moodiness and irritability because of worries about grades and friends
10 **(4th–5th Grades)**	• Content • Responsible • Usually truthful • Works well in groups	• Better anger control • Compliant
11 **(5th–6th Grades)**	• Abrasive • Argumentative • Intrusive • Stubborn • Expects perfection from adults	• Self-centered • Rude • Protests rules • Purposeful forgetting • Moody
12 **(6th–7th Grades)**	• Energetic • Enthusiastic • Many psychosexual changes • Minds reluctantly • Emphatic • Insightful	• Productive activities (grades, music, sports) • Better problem-solving skills
13 **(7th–8th Grades)**	• Many physical changes of a sexual nature • Verbally explosive • Developing new friendships • Self-preoccupied • Quiet	• Beginning abstract thinking • Irritable • Dissatisfied • Stronger peer pressure to conform
14 **(8th–9th Grades)**	• More outgoing • Much more verbal • Easily bored • Critical	• More active social life • Active interest in sexual matters
15 **(9th–10th Grades)**	• Rejection of family (doesn't want to be seen with them) • Sexual preoccupations • Isolationist (stays in room at home) • Highly critical of all adults	• Caught in the middle of childhood and adulthood (not as secure and dependent as children, and not as confident and mature as adults)
16 and Older **(10th–12th Grades)**	• More inner peace • Conflicts regarding peer popularity • Identity	• More self-confident • Improved social skills for getting along with adults • Career and vocational choice

 From *The Seven Habits of Peaceful Parents* by Dr. Joseph Cress, Dr. Elizabeth Lonning, and Burt Berlowe. **Handout 11**

Active Listening Stems

- "You sound _____"

- "You feel _____"

- "You would really like to _____"

- "It sounds as if you're feeling _____"

- "It seems you're _____"

"I" Message Statements

Begin with the word "I" followed by a "feeling" word such as:

- "I feel annoyed when you don't come home on time."

Change questions into statements. For example:

- "What time did you get home last night?" becomes "The clock showed 1:45 A.M. when you came home. This is past curfew and we need to talk about it."

 From *The Seven Habits of Peaceful Parents* by Dr. Joseph Cress, Dr. Elizabeth Lonning, and Burt Berlowe.

Feeling Words

Positive

Adventurous	High	
Affection	Honored	
Alert	Hopeful	
Alive	Inquisitive	
Amazed	Inspired	
Amused	Intense	
Appreciation	Interested	
Aroused	Intrigued	
Astonished	Invigorated	
Bold	Involved	
Buoyant	Joyous	
Calm	Jubilant	
Capable	Keyed-up	
Carefree	Loving	
Challenged	Mellow	
Cheerful	Merry	
Clever	Optimistic	
Comfortable	Overjoyed	
Complacent	Overwhelmed	
Concerned	Peaceful	
Confident	Pleasant	
Contented	Pretty	
Cool	Proud	
Curious	Quiet	
Dazzled	Radiant	
Delighted	Refreshed	
Eager	Relieved	
Ecstatic	Satisfied	
Elated	Secure	
Electrified	Spellbound	
Encouraged	Splendid	
Enjoyable	Stimulated	
Enlivened	Sure	
Enthusiastic	Surprised	
Exalted	Tenderness	
Excited	Thankful	
Exhilarated	Thrilled	
Exuberant	Touched	
Fascinated	Tranquil	
Free	Trusting	
Friendly	Warm	
Fulfilled		
Glad		
Glowing		
Grateful		
Groovy		
Happy		

Negative

Abandoned	Displeased	Melancholy
Afraid	Dissatisfied	Miserable
Aggravated	Distressed	Mopy
Agitated	Disturbed	Nervous
Alarmed	Divided	Odd
Aloof	Downcast	Overwhelmed
Amazed	Edgy	Perplexed
Ambivalent	Embarrassed	Pessimistic
Angry	Embittered	Pleasant
Anguished	Envious	Provoked
Animosity	Exasperated	Puzzled
Annoyed	Exhausted	Reluctant
Anxious	Fatigued	Repelled
Apathetic	Fearful	Resentful
Apprehensive	Fidgety	Restless
Aroused	Foolish	Righteous
Aversion	Frightened	Sad
Bad	Frustrated	Scared
Beat	Furious	Shaky
Betrayed	Glad	Shocked
Bitter	Gloomy	Skeptical
Blah	Guilty	Sorrowful
Blue	Hate	Sorry
Bored	Helpless	Spiritless
Brokenhearted	Hesitant	Surprised
Burdened	Horrible	Terrified
Chagrined	Horrified	Thwarted
Cold	Hostile	Tired
Competitive	Hurt	Troubled
Condemned	Impatient	Ugly
Confused	Indifferent	Uncomfortable
Contented	Infuriated	Unconcerned
Cross	Inquisitive	Uneasy
Crushed	Insecure	Unhappy
Curious	Insensitive	Unnerved
Dejected	Irate	Unsteady
Depressed	Irked	Upset
Despondent	Irritated	Uptight
Detached	Isolated	Vexed
Disappointed	Jealous	Vulnerable
Discouraged	Jittery	Worried
Disgruntled	Lazy	Wretched
Disgusted	Let-down	
Disheartened	Listless	
Disinterested	Lonely	
Dislike	Mad	
Dismay	Mean	

 From *The Seven Habits of Peaceful Parents* by Dr. Joseph Cress, Dr. Elizabeth Lonning, and Burt Berlowe.

Communication Exercises

Parent-Child

1. A child leaves the bathroom a mess after taking a bath. Water and toys are everywhere. The parent blows up and starts yelling at the child.

2. The children are bickering over who gets to hold the TV remote control. The parent gets upset, shuts the TV off, and sends them to their rooms.

3. A child will not get dressed and ready for school in the morning. You have gotten her up and prompted her three or four times to please get ready to go. Each time you give a directive, "Put your socks on," she replies, "No, I don't want to," and your anger level rises with each prompt.

4. Your family has been invited to a wedding and you've decided to go. It involves traveling a fair distance in the car, so you prepare your children and bring along activities for them during the drive. The journey goes well and you're feeling positive about it all. However, when you start out for the church, misbehavior begins to flare. They talk very loudly, don't want to sit still, and are generally unruly.

Parent-Teen

1. A teen comes home three hours after the agreed-on curfew. The parent yells and grounds the teen from everything for a month.

2. A teen comes home and has obviously been drinking. The parent explodes and calls the local substance-abuse program and demands the adolescent be admitted to the inpatient program.

3. Your 15-year-old son, who is too young to have a driver's license, takes the family car and picks up some friends to "go cruising." He is home by his curfew and doesn't understand why he is being punished, since he was on time and he returned everyone home safely. He becomes argumentative and angry, lashes out verbally, and begins to stomp around slamming doors in protest.

4. You and your spouse have gone away for a quiet weekend to reconnect as spouses. You have a great time and return home feeling rejuvenated. When you walk in the door, you notice there has been a party. Your teenagers are sleeping and you become very angry, feeling betrayed, as you wake them up, yelling about their breaking their word and letting you down.

From *The Seven Habits of Peaceful Parents* by Dr. Joseph Cress, Dr. Elizabeth Lonning, and Burt Berlowe.

Ground Rules
For Family Meetings

1. The person speaking should be respected and not interrupted.

2. Family members need to be under control at all times.

3. Family members need to use "I" statements.

Important vs. Urgent Quadrant Sheet

	Urgent	Not Urgent
Important	• Accident • Health crisis • Some misbehavior • Poor grades • Low self-esteem • Problems with alcohol, drugs, sex, smoking • Study for big test tomorrow • Truancy • Driving • Some 900 number calls • Legal problems	• Dealing with values, respect • Discussing sexuality • Playing board games, cards, etc. • Teaching skills like sewing, baking, changing tires, changing oil • Family meetings • Planning • Working on our reactions to their provocative behavior
Not Important	• Spilled milk • Dog accident • Ringing phone • Interruptions • Some phone calls • Drop-in visits • Laundry • Messy rooms • Getting up on time • Some music selections • Some clothing issues • Some hairstyles	• Many phone calls • TV • Reading junk mail • Busywork • Some shopping • Haircuts • Some baking, mending • Most hairstyles

	Urgent	Not Urgent
Important		
Not Important		

From *The Seven Habits of Peaceful Parents* by Dr. Joseph Cress, Dr. Elizabeth Lonning, and Burt Berlowe.

Positive Feedback

Beneficial

"Jim, I appreciate your helping out with vacuuming. This means we can go to the park sooner."

"The garage looks great. Thanks for sweeping the floor."

Less Beneficial

"Kate, thanks for being such a good girl."

"Thanks for always helping out."

Corrective Feedback 1

Allows a Child to Feel Valued and Loved

"Billy, the car got scratched because you rode your bike too close to it. This makes extra work for me to fix it. Next time, walk your bike when you are near the car."

Detracts from a Child Feeling Valued and Loved

"Billy, you scratched the car because you didn't listen. How many times have I told you not to ride your bike near the car? Don't you ever listen?"

Corrective Feedback 2

Allows a Child to Feel Responsible and Competent

Five-year-old Molly is excitedly passing out cupcakes at her birthday party and two fall on the floor. Mom says, "Thanks for helping out, Molly. We've got plenty of extras."

Detracts from a Child Feeling Responsible and Confident

Five-year-old Molly is excitedly passing out cupcakes at her birthday party and two fall on the floor. Mom says, "Here, Molly, let me do it. You're just too young to help out."

Social Skills

- Personal introductions

- Beginning a conversation

- Joining in a conversation

- Ending a conversation

- Giving a compliment

- Accepting a compliment

- Offering to help a friend

- Sharing

- Apologizing

- Recognizing other people's feelings

- Dealing with anger

- Dealing with other people's anger

- Dealing with fear

- Asking permission

- Dealing with teasing

- Dealing with accusations

- Dealing with losing

- Dealing with being left out

- Dealing with failure

 From *The Seven Habits of Peaceful Parents* by Dr. Joseph Cress, Dr. Elizabeth Lonning, and Burt Berlowe.

The Relationship Savings Account

Examples of Deposits

- Compliments
- Positive attention
- Sharing
- Hug
- Smile
- "I Love You"
- Reflective listening
- Surprise presents

Examples of Withdrawals

- Name calling
- Yelling
- Sarcasm
- Ridicule
- Physical restraint

Signs of a Full Account

- Child shows affection
- Child shares
- Child complies
- Child seeks help from parent

Signs of an Empty, Bankrupt Account

- Parents have unrealistic expectations
- Explosive outbursts
- Noncompliance
- Name calling
- Sarcasm

 From *The Seven Habits of Peaceful Parents* by Dr. Joseph Cress, Dr. Elizabeth Lonning, and Burt Berlowe. **Handout 19**

Model Statements

- I like it when we play nicely together.

- It is nice when you help clean up.

- That was a terrific tower you just built.

- You did that all by yourself.

- You really acted grown-up when you didn't get upset when your plan didn't work out.

 From *The Seven Habits of Peaceful Parents* by Dr. Joseph Cress, Dr. Elizabeth Lonning, and Burt Berlowe.

Ten Parent-Child Situations

Decide whether the parent's comment is a "deposit" or a "withdrawal."

1. Six-year-old Chris snatches a toy car away from his younger brother. His father says, "Chris, quit being so selfish. If you don't share, you can go to your room!"

2. Eight-year-old Katy says, "When I grow up I want to be just like you, Mom." Mom answers, "That would really be neat."

3. Eleven-year-old twins complain about dinner again. Their mom replies, "One more comment like that and you can both go to bed right now."

4. Christie, age nine, gets her new white shirt all full of paint during art class. Her mom says, "It looks as though you had a fun time at art class. It might be a good idea to wash your shirt now before the paint dries."

5. Mark comes home from school complaining about his teacher and calling him names. His father says, "It sounds as though you're really upset with your teacher today. What happened?"

6. Brian tells his parents that he hates them and wishes he never had them as parents. His father answers, "Don't ever talk to me like that again. If you do, you will regret it."

7. Peggy, age seven, wet her bed again. Her father says, "When are you going to grow up? Only babies wet their beds."

8. Eight-year-old Jeff left his bike in the driveway again. Dad says, "I almost ran over your bike again. I'm going to put it in the garage, and I don't want you to ride it for a day. In the meantime, we have to come up with a better place to leave it."

9. Kari is in sixth grade and doesn't understand how to do her math homework. Her mother says, "I can't believe you can't do those problems. How will you ever graduate from high school?"

10. Twelve-year-old Mary tried to clean up her room, but it still looks messy. Her father says, "That's a big job. Let's work together. Sometimes it's easier that way."

Expectations

1. Eight-year-old Jessica and her six-year-old brother Tommy fight incessantly. They bicker at every meal, refuse to share toys, and often call each other bad names. At times they hit, kick, and bite each other.

2. Jeremy is ten and he still sucks his thumb, wets his bed, and needs someone to tie his shoes.

3. Brian is nine years old and forgets to take care of his bike. He often forgets where he leaves it. Sometimes he just dumps it on the driveway. Twice his parents nearly ran over it.

4. Jimmy, age five, tells his mother that he hates her and wishes that he had someone else for a mother.

5. Ten-year-old Beth has a messy room. Her clothes are never put away; books and dolls are everywhere. Apple cores, empty pop cans, and candy wrappers litter the floor.

6. Eleven-year-old Charity is slow to mind. Whenever her parents ask her to do something she says, "In a minute." This minute becomes hours, and very little gets done.

7. Scott, age nine, has lots of behavior problems at school. He started a fight at recess and is often disrespectful toward teachers.

8. Eleven-year-old Jimmy doesn't always tell the truth. He usually tells his parents that he has no homework, but later they receive notes from his teacher wondering why he didn't turn work in. He says that a friend gave him a yo-yo, but the parents later learn that he stole it. He denies doing things his parents know for certain that he's done.

9. Peggy, age twelve, is easily discouraged. She complains that she has no friends at school, that she is the worst soccer player, that she receives bad grades, and that nothing ever goes right in her life.

10. It's bedtime, and nine-year-old Kelly begins her avoidance strategies. She insists she has to finish watching a TV program, get a drink, find a special stuffed animal, go to the bathroom one more time.

From *The Seven Habits of Peaceful Parents* by Dr. Joseph Cress, Dr. Elizabeth Lonning, and Burt Berlowe.

Parent Pre/Post Test

T or F   1. Controlling negative emotions, especially anger, is an essential skill for parents.

T or F   2. Parents should be able to reason with children by the time the children are even years of age.

T or F   3. For most challenging childhood behavior, there is no one right solution; many solutions may work equally well.

T or F   4. Most behavioral programs for children will be successful if the parents are consistent for five to seven days.

T or F   5. Parents need to spend at least thirty minutes of quality time with each child daily.

T or F   6. Most important things in life are urgent.

T or F   7. Parents can nurture a child's self-esteem by helping a child feel loved and competent.

T or F   8. In using corrective feedback, use plenty of words to make sure you get the message across.

T or F   9. Global positive praise is just as helpful as specific positive feedback.

T or F   10. The quantity and quality of affection messages a child sends to parents are a measure of the amount of goodwill in the child-parent bank account.

     Handout 23

Parent Satisfaction Measure

The following six statements are related to the peaceful parenting program. Please rate the sentences (1–6) in the space to the right.

1. Completely Agree
2. Mostly Agree
3. Somewhat Agree
4. Somewhat Disagree
5. Mostly Disagree
6. Completely Disagree

1. The location, room, and arrangements were satisfactory. _____

2. I was treated respectfully by all the staff. _____

3. I feel the sessions improved my parenting skills. _____

4. The facilitator was helpful in presenting meaningful material. _____

5. The topics, experiences, and sharing were helpful. _____

6. I would recommend the program to a friend. _____

Facilitator
Self-Assessment

1. Were all parents introduced to each other and did all seem to be comfortable?

2. Were the room, schedule, arrangements, and topics helpful in meeting the parents' goals?

3. Was I able to complete the session within the time frame?

4. Was I able to encourage all parents to participate by sharing their experiences, opinions, and insights?

From *The Seven Habits of Peaceful Parents* by Dr. Joseph Cress, Dr. Elizabeth Lonning, and Burt Berlowe. **Handout 25**

Behavioral Plan

Name of Child _____ Date Started _____

1. Specific negative behavior to be decreased:

2. Consequences:

3. Incompatible positive behavior to be increased (optional):

4. Consequences (optional):

 From *The Seven Habits of Peaceful Parents* by Dr. Joseph Cress, Dr. Elizabeth Lonning, and Burt Berlowe.